Tribals of Manipur and Modernisation

Tribals of Manipur and Modernisation

Salam Irene
Ginneiching Simte
Thenkhogin Haokip

Maulana Abul Kalam Azad Institute of Asian Studies, Kolkata

Anshah Publishing House

ISBN: 978-81-8364-095-4

First Published in India in 2014

Tribals of Manipur and Modernisation

Published by:
ANSHAH PUBLISHING HOUSE
LG, Pankaj Central Market, I.P. Ext.,
Patparganj, Delhi-110092, Tel: 22235152, 9810522367
Br.Off. 4617/18, Ansari Road, Darya Ganj,
New Delhi-110002, Tel: 9650028065

Preface

Manipur is a small landlocked state located on the International boundary between India and Myanmar. Because of its geo-strategic location, waves of migrants have been coming to the state and making it their home as e.g. the two waves of Kukis- the 'old' and 'new' as also the Nagas tribes. The predominant tribal population of Manipur can be broadly divided into two the Naga and the Kuki. These nomenclatures include a vast number of tribes within their fold, many of whom are now asserting a separate identity.

Despite historical, social, cultural affinities with the people of South East and East Asia, Manipur, a sovereign kingdom till the advent of colonial rule in 1891, remained comparatively isolated from the outside world with the exception of Burma, as it was constantly at war with that country. This isolation bred insularity, which hampered even the British attempts prior to 1891 to established western education in Manipur.

But a sea change was affected when Manipur came under British domination in 1891. The British believed that it was their bounden duty to tame the hill tribes of Manipur and rid them of practices such as head hunting and worship of nature, animal sacrifice etc., they were assisted by the Christian missionaries who in a few short decades converted almost the entire tribal population to Christianity. They were able to do so because it was they who modernized the tribal by exposing them not only to the Gospel of Christ, but to the western system of education. Their efforts were facilitated by the British Political Agents who themselves benefitted from missionary activity.

The impact of modernization was evident in every activity of the tribals in Manipur- in sphere of education, literacy, vocational learning, standard of living, hygiene, spread of urbanization, cash crop production, emergence of a middle class abandonment of indigenous forms of worship, dress, language, fine-arts, and religion. The emergence of a middle class, educated in the new learning, gave rise to a class of professionals: bureaucrats, politicians, doctors, engineers, businessmen, lawyers, priests, nurses, academicians, who began to dominate to a great extent the politics and government of state, its business, trade, commerce, education, religion etc. The twin factors of western education and Christian missionary activity broadened the world of the tribals of Manipur and produced basic changes in their social and cultural life. This was made possible because Christianity being a community oriented religion was in harmony with the classless, service oriented society of the tribals. But from a primitive society subsisting on shifting cultivation, tribal society was catapulted forward to grapple with modern ideas, technologies and way of life. The transition was explosive not gradual, but it induced so much that was clearly for the good of the people. The church was one of the most important agencies of social change. This is especially evident in the rise in the standard of living of the tribals, following the introduction of western education. It also taught the tribals to commit their rich oral history to a written script. However the increase in urbanization led many tribals to abandon their old value system and traditional forms of behavior. In their first wave of enthusiasm under the new faith, they abandoned many rich cultural treasures, in the realm of music, dance, feasting etc. The effect of modernization also ushered in the concepts of both individualism and a consumerist culture, and weakened traditional family and clan bonds. There can be no doubt that Christianity and education transformed tribal society and its momentum has been sustained by the focus of the Christian missionaries in recent decades on Inculturation, Mission and Contextualization.

Education introduced the tribals to a new world, and rid them of the fear of superstitious belief, as also expenses involved in traditional rituals like Feast of Merit. It provided new opportunities for sustainable livelihood, especially in government services, the tribals became more advanced and progressive, and girls' education was viewed as a means to empower women. An inadvertent effect of modernization resulting from education and Christianity was the emergence of a middle class which changed the balance of power in tribal society making the position of tribal chiefs non-essential and redundant. It was the middle class who assumed the reins of leadership and whose way of life became a benchmark to be emulated by others. Colonial administration ushered in new concepts/institutions of administration and jurisprudence, a money economy, a westernized lifestyle new ideology- which a few decades later led to an assertion of ethnic identity. The British had popularized the terms 'Kuki' and 'Naga' creating a common identity since the early 9th century for their own purposes and convenience.

Globalisation too impacted tribal life and culture. It caused tribals to migrate to urban areas where they imbibed new ideas which enabled them to rise to the highest positions in politics and society. It also introduced the tribals to commercialization of their agrarian economy, improved production of goods and service, introduction of new technologies especially in the field of IT, and communication and awareness of human rights. In this process of modernization /globalization an erosion of ethnic culture occurred and a consumerist mindset was adopted by the people, especially tribals benefitting from cross border trade with Myanmar. A division occurred in society, between 'the have' and 'the have nots'. A liberal economy ushered in a drugs epidemic into the state followed soon by an explosion of the AIDS pandemic, and an increase in poppy cultivation.

Many middle class tribals migrated to metropolitan towns in India as also to other countries and formed a sizable diaspora. But remittances back to Manipur are few and far between. Also young tribals settled outside are raising the spectre of only a very young and very old tribal population being left behind in the state with no support system in place. By and large only those with money and muscle power are able to access employment opportunities in the government sector. Globalization has accelerated corruption and nepotism in the state.

The private sector has yet to develop, hindered as it is by a culture of violence endemic in the state continuous strikes impact even education and children sent out for education often fall prey to human trafficking.

Greater emphasis on ethnicity and nationalism have led to factional feuds and hampered development. It cannot be disputed however that the most important factors that ushered in modernization among Manipur's tribals were western education and Christianity.

Contents

Contents

Introduction

Manipur is a tiny State in the North Eastern region of India with its capital in the city of Imphal. It is a State bounded by the Indian States of Nagaland in the North, Mizoram in the South and Assam in the west. It also borders the country of Myanmar to the East. It lies between 23-83°N and 25.68°N latitude and 93.°3°E to 94.78° longitudes.

Manipur has a land surface of 22,347 sq.km. And about 90% of the land is mountainous. Manipur's scenic beauty, lakes and water bodies, craftsmanship, folkdances, and folklores, rich diverse, culture and traditions its recorded history in the Cheitharol Kumpapa makes it a unique land, which existed as an independent kingdom till the advent of Colonial rule in 1891.

Manipur literally means 'Jewelled land' nestled deep within the lush green corner of North East India. It seems much like an exquisite work of art executed by superb hands of Nature and is indeed a State of exquisite natural beauty and splendor, the beauty of which once inspired Mrs. St. Clair Grimwood who described it as "A pretty place more beautiful than many show places of the world". Even the Late Pandit Jawaharlal Nehru paid a fitting tribute by describing it as "the Jewel of India."

Manipur is a State inhabited by different Communities. Whereas the tribals are mainly concentrated and confined to the hill areas, the valley of Imphal is predominantly inhabited by the Meiteis, and is followed by the Meitei-Pangal, Non-Manipuris and a sizable proportion of tribals. During the reign of Garib Niwas, in the late eighteenth century, the process of Sanskritisation occurred in the valley, and consequently the Meitei-population converted enmasse to Hinduism. But this development left the tribals untouched. The factor, which has left the deepest imprint on the tribals in the last two centuries, has been the single factor of modernization. Modernization of the tribal communities is the result of the working of two forces viz., (a) The impact of Christianity, and (b) the introduction of western education. Both these two developments occurred almost simultaneously in the nineteenth century and pre-dated the British Colonial occupation of Manipur (1891). They gained momentum in the twentieth century. The result of modernization has entailed great expenditure and investments in the public spheres (construction of schools, colleges, vocational and I.T.I. centres, improvement in mode and means of communication and transport to name a few). Far-reaching changes have also taken place in the sphere of politics, society, culture and religion.

The people of Manipur are grouped into three main ethnic communities: the Meiteis, who inhabit the valley and the 33 major tribes in the hills, which are further, divided into two main ethno-denominations namely Nagas and Kuki-Chins. The Meiteis are themselves divided into the Meiteis (the natives in the valley), Bamon (originally of Bengal Brahmin origin) and Meitei Pangans (originally migrants from Sylhet/Cachar). They all speak Meiteilon. In addition to the Meiteis, the valley is also inhabited by Nepalis, Bengalis, Marwaris and many people from other Indian communities. At present people from the hills have also migrated and settled in the valley.

The Naga group consists of Zeliangrong (which is composed of three related tribes namely Rongmei, Liangmei and Zemei), Tangkhul, Mao, Maram, Paomei, Maring, Moyon,

Anal Monsang, Tarao, and Chothe, Koireng, Lamgang, Thangal. At present, these Nagas groups inhibit major parts of Ukhrul district, Senapati district, Tamenglong district and Chandel district.

The Chin-Kuki group consists of Tedim Chin (officially recognized by the Indian Union as Sukte), Gangte, Simte, Hmar, Paite, Thadou, Vaiphei, Zou, Mate etc. These groups of people are major inhabitants of the districts of Churachandpur, Chandel and Sadar Hills Sub-divisions. They are also scattered all over the other districts as well. The term Chin is used for the people in the neighbouring Chin State of Myanmar whereas Chins are called Kukis on the Indian Side. Some Kuki groups like Paite, Vaiphei, Zou, Simte etc. recently identify themselves as Zomi and have distanced themselves from the name Kuki. Thadous remain as the major Kuki tribe in the Chin-Kuki group.

The erstwhile kingdom of Manipur though witness to several migrations into the kingdom from the countries of south east Asia and parts of India, nevertheless remained isolated from its neighbors, practically unchanged up to 1891, when the colonial administration opened it up to western culture, education and Christian missionary activity. It therefore developed a kind of insularity in various spheres, which hampered development particularly in the field of education and literacy. In fact, the kings of Manipur did not afford patronage to education and only a rudimentary life value form of education was imparted to the people with emphasis on household management for women and girls and military training for boys and men. There also existed the feudal lallup system, which entailed mandatory ten days service out of every forty days for all male adults to the king. The state had a predominant agrarian economy but as the army was constantly engaged in warfare, it was the women, who managed the economy of the state and set up markets at convenient spots on the wayside. In fact, in the capital Imphal, there was an exclusive women's market known as "Ima keithel". This acted not only as a centre of market transactions, but also as a platform forum for women to come together and express and assert their aspirations and forge strategies to solve complex socio-economic problems. As there was sufficient product for the populace, they were not much concerned about what was occurring in the regions surrounding them, although they were rudely awakened by the consequences of the Seven Years Devastation, 1819-1826. Even after the Burmese left Manipur, the people continued with their traditional occupations centering mainly on agriculture, spinning and weaving.

From the first quarter of the nineteenth century, the British began to establish relations with the erstwhile kingdom of Manipur. The treaty of Yandaboo 1826 marked a historic milestone in relations between the Manipuris and the British. As per the Treaty, Manipur was placed under the protection of British officials with payment of taxes in return. And Gambhir Singh was recognized as Raja of Manipur. Both the British and the King of Burma gave recognition to the independence of Manipur.

The British first tried to establish a school on the line of western education in Manipur for the first time. Captain Gordon, who was the Political Agent, after obtaining permission from the Maharaja Chandrakirti opened a school on 1837 at his own expense. He tried his best to popularise the school. He even compiled one English-Bengali Manipuri dictionary. But his enthusiasm and sincere effort to establish the school was rendered futile, as the school had to close down, partly due to the fact that people had a false notion, that they would become sahibs in due course, eat even beef, mutton etc, and lose their caste if they availed themselves of an English education. After the closure of this school for a long period of 34 years, no attempts to open a school, was made by the government or any individual officer or by the public.

The second attempt was made by W. F. Nuthal, the Political Agent, after obtaining permission from the King. He opened a vernacular school in 1872 at Langthabal, at his own expense. At the beginning, a few boys attended the school occasionally. The rulers again, never showed any enthusiasm or desire for the progress of the school, as they were aware that if literary education was not patronized by them, they would be able to maintain the existing status quo in society, administration and economics. The people also showed no interest in availing themselves of the opportunity of education on the western pattern, as many high officials themselves, were unable to read or write. Children naturally, having received no encouragement from parents, preferred the age old past time of playing, especially kangjei or foot hockey by boys. Once again, for lack of encouragement, on the part both of the rulers and the public, the school had to be closed down indefinitely.

Twelve years later, the same idea of establishing a school was mooted by Sir James Johnstone, Political Agent in Manipur from 1877 to 1886. He immediately put forward a proposal to the King for permission to open an English school in Imphal, but his request was greeted with silence. He too became despondent, in the end, with the help of some ministers, Thangal Major-General, Sawaijamba Menjor and Rama Singh; he obtained permission from the King to open a school. Immediately, he started a Middle English school in1885 named after him in the residency compound. This was the start of the gradual growth in western education in Manipur, which received its fill up from Christian missionaries in later years.

Almost simultaneously with the attempts at western education, was the advent of the Christian missionaries. It was under these circumstances that William Pettigrew approached Mr. A. Portious, the acting Political Agent, (as the Political Agent Major Maxwell was on furlough) and started his work at Imphal, the capital of the state, on 6th February 1894. He set out to spread literacy on western lines among the masses. He began a private tuition class, which however consisted only of the children of Government servants. Dissatisfied with this, he then in consultation with the State authorities opened an ideal school at Moirangkhom in Imphal, which later came to be known as the Pettigrew School. He wrote a Manipuri grammar, compiled an English-Bengali-Manipuri dictionary and some other books and taught Manipuri in his school.

Pettigrew began to think that his calling was among the Meiteis and was anxious to preach the Gospel among them. But the Hinduised Meiteis construed Pettigrew's preaching as a deliberate attempt to impose upon them the 'government's religion'. Maxwell, the Political Agent on his return from furlough, took an alarming view of the new emergent situation and expressed his fear that trouble might arise if Pettigrew's activities were not nipped in the bud because the Meiteis held on to the tenets of the Hindu religion almost to the point of fanaticism. Thus the Maharaja envisaged some kind of hostile reaction to Pettigrew's work in the valley, The Political Agent was compelled to ask Pettigrew to leave the valley but allowed him to shift his work to the hills.

Pettigrew was sadly disappointed because the door for missionary work in Manipur was closed. Maxwell came to his rescue and suggested that he should work in the hill areas as the British were taken aback at some of the cultural practices of the hill tribes as for example head-hunting, which established a warrior's Prowers and wanted to bring about reforms in many of the socio-cultural practices of the local people, including the brewing of rice beer and rice wine, which rendered the people inebriated on various occasions and festivals.

Until recent times, the people of Manipur have been quite isolated and the land very remote and far from the modern and technological advancements. However, with the coming of the British rule in India, innovations and changes occurred in every field and the kingdom was put on the path of modernization. The British administrators and colonialists however thought it their bourden duty to rid the hill tribes of the barbaric practice of head-hunting and other primitive rituals.

The tribals of Manipur professed different religions and spoke different languages. They frequently quarreled amongst themselves and head-hunting was a dominant practice. They believed in the presence of innumerable spirits. These spirits were believed to reside in trees, rivers lakes, springs, and caves, holes in the earth, salt springs, rocks, waterfalls, cliffs, animals and human bodies. They thought that sickness and misfortunes of any kind were the work of evil spirits. It was even believed that the spirits could make appearances before people, and terrifying stories were told about such occurrences. They, therefore, offered different kinds of sacrifices, which required shedding of animal's blood, as prescribed by the priest. Sacrifices to appease the evil spirits were made through Puithiem/Siampu (priest). But, this does not mean that they were worshippers of evil spirits. They did this out of fear and out of their desire to get rid of their sickness. They have been serious and sincere in their religious beliefs and practices. However deep within them they had a belief running through their veins that there was one true God, who was the Supreme Being, the Creator and the Lord of the whole world. They practiced rituals and sacrifices to please the lesser gods and the Almighty too. They worshipped natural deities and made sacrifices and offerings to propitiate Gods as also evils spirits. In their quest for the Supreme Being, they spent much time, energy and devotion in the practice of their indigenous religions. But their mode of worship tended to fuse them into a homogenous community, where rituals and gennas were rigidly observed.

People were simple and God fearing, honest and hardworking. No doubt they could be ruthless in war but in times of peace, they lived together in harmony and contentment, and they were relatively free of greed and avarice as they had no contact with the outside world and so never pined for costly, worldly goods. They were happy if they were blessed with a bountiful harvest.

Being worshippers of nature, people were inclined towards superstition and lived in fear that if they were unable to please the Gods and spirits, the wrath of the latter would descend upon them. In their ignorance, they ascribed any calamity to God's wrath. When the Christian missionaries preached faith in one God, who is a loving father, and who made no distinction between one man and another, the tribals, began to embrace the new religion though they manifested some resistance in the beginning.

Instead of strong opposition and resistance at the beginning of the missionary activities, hill tribes began to accept Christ gradually as their personal savior and Lord. They were happy to accept Jesus Christ as the son of the Almighty God. They found God could save them from the crippling power of the evil spirits whom they used to often appease with sacrifices. When people realized that only Christ could set them free from this fearful life and bondage to evil spirits and demons, they began to embrace this new faith of Christianity.

When they accepted this new faith in Christ, they believed that the powerful Spirit of God was always with them, which ensured them security in their lives. In their old traditional faiths, their lives were full of fear, there were certain places such as big trees, rocks, dense forests, riversides, and graveyards, which they believed the devils, inhabited. They observed different kinds of gennas and taboos in order to attain a good life in this world.

They forsook their old faith and way of living and discontinued their practice of drinking wine and rice-beer, divination, sorcery, necromancy, sacrifices to evil Spirits, observance of gennas and taboos. They realized that they were no longer under oppression from evil spirits and demons, but were emancipated in Christ. They found peace in Him and believed in His promise of eternal life.

Through a process of acculturation, the missionaries coming from the west established an affinity with the hill people. They learnt their language, their ways of life. Above all, they made Manipur their home and in course of time, they were not only accepted but welcomed by the local populace.

The missionaries gradually acquainted themselves with the lifestyles of local tribals, ate their food and learned their languages. They lived in the community, as did the tribals and exhibited great care for the people. As time passed, the tribals began to discard their doubts and suspicions about the foreigners and started listening to their preaching. Once the missionaries were accepted in the localities, their words and teachings found ready acceptance among the populace. Before introducing the new faith, the missionaries concentrated on explaining the rationale behind the superstitions that had held the people in thrall. They afforded rational explanations, and in a relatively short span of time, the tribals realized that there were no benign or malignant spirits, and so they freed themselves of fear, and listened attentively to the Gospel message, which brought revolutionary changes in their socio-religious life. Thus, the tribals of Manipur began to place their faith in the missionaries and their teachings.

In the realm of religion, Christianity has replaced the primeval religion of the tribals, which focused on the worship mainly of nature. Evangelization was born of transfiguring religious experience – this experience was the experience of conversion, of being born again, but the missionaries were of the view that, 'Culture is the vital space within which the human, person comes face to face with the Gospel'. The Christian missionaries aim at contextualization of the message of Christ i.e. clothing Jesus and His message in the idiom and language of the people. In the initial stages of evangelization, however, many Christian missionaries described the culture of the tribals as heathen and pagan. With this faulty understanding of culture, many missionaries were instrumental in throwing away the cultural expression of people, especially their dances, festivals, beliefs, folklore, folksongs etc. With education, the tribals felt angry at the insensitivity of the missionaries, and also uneasy with the speed of westernization, that invaded their territory.

The Christian missionaries also taught the people many things, the Gospel, reading, writing, rudimentary arithmetic, health care, personal hygiene, nutrition, vocational arts and so on. This changed the outlook of the tribal people who appreciated the rise in their standard of living that imparted quality to their lives. In fact, the modernization of the tribals commenced with the establishment of western education and their conversion to Christianity. They were taught English, so that they would be able to read the Bible and sing hymns in church. This familiarized the people with the English tongue, enabling the tribals to quickly establish a superior fluency in the language.

The main impact of Christianity was felt in the sphere of education because although the primary focus of Christian mission in Manipur was the propagation of the Gospel. Almost consequent upon their arrival in Manipur, they established schools, thus bringing light, knowledge and literacy to the hitherto illiterate tribals of Manipur. This spread of education was facilitated by the British Political Agent but the latter's success in the field was minimal. The Christian schools imparted learning, moral and spiritual values, and pursued cultural goals and the human formation of youth. They taught man in his totality, in relation to God and in relation to the world. Since the efforts of the missionaries were directed towards human advancement, especially among the poor and abandoned youth, they contributed in a significant manner in not only appreciably raising the level of literacy but also the standard of living. Since they opened dispensaries, orphanages, medical centres, hospitals, hospices, they not only treated the sick and needy, but also taught hygiene and remedies for minor ailments, while they inculcated in the tribals, a sense of self- reliance, as also responsibility. The tribals under the impact of Christianity abandoned their traditional dormitories (the crucibles in which youth were moulded into men). They unfortunately replaced community values with individualism and consumerism. As a result of modernization, for instance, self- sufficiency in rice cultivation was replaced largely in some tribal areas with cash crop plantations. All these changes radically impacted and changed the identity of society, as also of the economy.

The impact of modernization and introduction of western education, enabled the tribals to take advantage of new opportunities that come with learning, and in course of time, a new class emerged in tribal society- a middle class comprised mainly of bureaucrats, police and army officers, teachers, doctors, nurses, lawyers, theologians, pharmacists, writers, scientists and scholars both among the people of the hills and valley. They controlled the politics, government, business, trade and commerce, education and culture of the state. The emergence of a powerful media, both print and electronic, led to the formation of a strong and alert public opinion more or less controlled by the middle class. Media controlled the thought of men. The peasantry both in the valley and the hills emerged quite powerful. Because of their larger numbers, they began to dominate the democratic process illustrated by the fact that political leaders from the rural areas began to dominate over the urban group in the control of the democratic political process, With reference to the tribals, to cite an example, Mr. T. N. Haokip a rural tribal peasant became a Minister. However today, demographic patterns have changed, and many rural tribal politicians now live in the urban centres, especially the capital town of Imphal. They only visit their rural constituencies when prudence bids them and of course for electioneering campaigns.

The religious belief that binds the people, which also facilitated the spread of the gospel, was the belief in life after death. They believe that the soul of the deceased goes to the 'Land of the Dead', which the Tangkhuls call 'Kazeiram', the Maos call 'Kathimei Raloku' and the Kukis-chins call 'Mithikhua/Misikhua'. It is their belief that in the world of the dead, there is an exact repetition of the life in this world. So the soul of the deceased goes to his or her own family in the Land of the Dead. As a matter of fact, the Tangkhuls practice the presentation of a gift to the dead. When a relative dies, a present is brought to the deceased person telling him or her to give it to his family members who died before and are already in the Land of the Dead. And all the friends and relatives give presents of various kinds to the dead person so as to help him continue his life journey to another world. They believe that the soul of a good person will go to heaven to live with the Supreme–God.

The tribals community believed in life after death even before Christianity arrived. There were two places where the spirit was supposed to live in the spirit world. Where the spirit of the departed one's would spend eternity was determined by the virtue and achievement of the dead person while living on earth. The spirit worlds were called Misikhua/Mithikhuo-village of the dead, Pialgal/Pielral-Paradise.

Misikhua – The spirits of most people were believed to go to misikhua, the village of the dead. It is the abode of the commoner's souls. This abode is believed to be located underground, very similar to the Hebrew concept of Sheol. It was believed the dead would unite again with their families who were already departed before them and earn their living like they did here on earth. All the slaves they have captured and the enemies they have killed would serve them as their servants in the place. The spirits of infants, on the other hand, may have hard time in finding out the way to misikhua. So when the infant dies, they would bury the body with an egg on his or her palm so that the egg would roll on toward misikhua and the child would follow the egg and reach the place.

When a man dies, his soul finds it very hard to adopt the life there. He is lonesome and comes to a mountain called Hringlang Tlang, or Ngaiban tlang, the mountain where the living are visible. So the spirit was believed to leave the body and linger for about some months around its former home on earth. Only when his family living in the world performed a rite called thitin (the dead-departed rite) then the soul was actually able to depart from this mountain. Eventually, it comes to a place where there is stream called Luonglo Tui/Lungloh Tui (water for no more loneliness) where the spirit of the departed is divested of all feeling and the living go in peace. There after he plucks a beautiful flower called Hawilo Par (a flower for no more looking back/or no turning back flower), only then are the desires of the soul for the land of the living extinguished. Then the soul proceeds toward Misikhua. Another home of souls is

Pialgal/Pielral (Beyond the river pial/Paradise) an abode of bliss. It is the abode, which every individual desires and strives to enter. Those who go there need not to work for their living. They will be fed with rice and meat by fair maidens. According to tradition, three groups of people were privileged to enter. The first are the Lamzuihs/Hlamzuis that is those children who die in infancy. The second was young men who had sexual relations with either three virgin girls or seven women. The third are those girls who remained virgins until death. The fourth and the most important criteria that guaranteed direct or free passage to Pialgal/Pielral was Thangsuah/Thangsuo (A person with outstanding achievement/Accomplisher). There are two ways to achieve the status of Thangsuah. By killing one each of the following species of animals-barking deer, sambhur, bear, wild boar, wild mithun, wild elephant, tiger, lion, eagle and a poisonous serpent or killing a hundred beasts or chopping off the head of an enemy. The second one is by cultivating a thousand bushels of rice in one single year.

The tribals concept of two worlds for the dead- Pialral and Mithikhua, and the Christian belief of heaven and hell were not very similar. Nevertheless, the concept of Pialral and Mithikhua was transformed by the Christian teaching of Heaven and Hell. Thus Christianity altered the concept of eschatology too. Christianity offered salvation to all irrespective of wealth or lack of it, provided that the newly converted Christians followed the precepts of Jesus Christ.

If we analyze the history of Christianity in Manipur from the very beginning of Christianity, hope of eternal life after death became the central theme of their preaching, and this concept greatly appealed to the converted tribals. They helped in composing Christian songs, whose theme was redemption and eternal life. Moreover, they were afforded the opportunity of forging a new identity and acquiring a better means of livelihood. When the concept of Heaven and Hell was made known to them, they did not have any problem in accepting it since they were eager to go to heaven or Pialral, which was not previously possible at all except a few people who earned the title of Thangsuah (Accomplisher).

The hill people remained essentially outside the orbit of Hindu influence and caste based societal formation. With their diverse social alignments and group identities, there was high degree of fluidity and flexibility in the socio-cultural arena. Even the colonial authorities had taken up a policy of segregating the hill and plains people (the inner line regulation of 1873).

Several reasons may explain the fast growth and development of the church in Manipur. Donna Strom asserted that the British occupation of the region and the subsequent prohibition of head-hunting, infanticide, slavery, sorcery and other cultural practices weakened the structure of the tribal society. When they were no longer allowed to practice head-hunting, their hope of reaching the village of the dead when they died was completely shattered, they had believed that their spirits after death would be accompanied by the spirits of those whose heads they had hunted. But a story of Jesus who promises eternal life appeared to be a very attractive alternative to them.

Secondly, although they still continued to sacrifices the blood of chickens, goats or dogs to appease the evil spirits, the Christians abandoned sorcery and sacrifices to demons. The practice of sacrifice and sorcery were replaced by prayer to God and use of modern medicine. The advent of Christianity had an impact on both the Christians and non-Christians as well.

Thirdly, the free education provided by the missionaries was another causative factor. Up to the advent of the Christian missionaries, the tribal people were geared to a subsistence-geared existence. They were not literate; they had no awareness of the importance of formal education. The missionaries came and established schools to provide free education to the people.

Finally, the Christian message of love and freedom inculcated a spirit of love and trust between people of different villages and tribes that enabled them to coexist peacefully.

CONCLUSION

The tribals of Manipur were looked down if not as backward at least as primitive. Today, the story is different. The tribals have become very progressive and in fact exhibit independent thinking and action in various spheres. Dr. Horam writes, "Truly, it was the Christian missions which introduced the tribal to the comity of nations. The missionaries were responsible for both the good and bad effects of the modern civilization on the tribals life."

It is an open secret that neither the Manipur Maharajas nor the Chieftains who had practiced a system of governance of the hill tribes of Manipur could affect the changes that have occurred within a span of a century because of the efforts of the Christian missionaries.

If the tribals have reached a semblance of development, a sizable portion of credit should go to the untiring works of the western, native and the Indian Missionaries who have worked untiringly to take the tribals to new heights of progress and advancement, including the adoption of new scientific and intellectual technology.

Thus, the arrival of the missionaries with their establishment of Churches and Schools initiated a process of epoch-making changes.

One

The Coming of Christianity and Its Role in Modernisation

For centuries, the tribal people of North-East India lived in isolation from the outside world and they also had little inter-tribal contact[1]. But as a native tribal social scientist in Manipur phrases it: "An individual in tribal society finds it difficult to exist without the security of belonging to a group which will share his joys and sorrows and with whose well-being, he can identify his own. Tribal social life, particularly of Manipur, is basically a classless society and there is no social stratification. The tribals have no written history; therefore if they want to record their history in written form, they have to rely heavily on arts and culture, songs and dances, legends and stories".[2]

Though the tribal people of North-East India differ among themselves in many ways, they also have in common many structural and cultural characteristics. For example, among certain tribes, (i) A boy can marry the widow of his deceased brother. (ii) Many practices and methods of sacrifice are similar (iii) Inheritance follows the male line (iv) The eldest son is to succeed the father in the family responsibility (v) Father is the head of the family (vi) Tribal forefathers believed in a Supreme Being. They also had their own mother tongues, life styles, social structures, rites and rituals, values and so on, differing in many ways from those of the non-tribal social groups in the country. Many of them are today settled agriculturists but forest still forms much of their economic resource base. They have one thing in common, namely their protest culture against those external forces, which try today or tried in the past to subjugate them, as for example British colonialists.

Underpinning the different Naga tribes' social structures and permeating every aspect of their lives were the tribal religions, which despite tremendous local variations were fundamentally similar[3]. The Naga Cosmology would accommodate head hunting and correlated feasts of merit as a way of life[4]. Among the Nagas, their myths of origin are essentially charters for social institutions and actions, besides legitimizing traditional customs and belief systems. Indeed, their rituals and beliefs are symbolic statements about expansion, social order and solidarity. Mythic perception, no doubt, then, has definitely guided their life pattern so much so that the basic structure of social life was, before the Christian Proselytisation, determined by sacred constraints and till today the social units of their clans are still traced back to a mythical guise. This mythical core extends to rituals connected with man-land relations, economic activities, clan rights and social relationships. These are manifested through narratives contained in stories and ballads, which are primarily texts of Naga social structure and processes.

A Naga insists that any deviation or incorrectness would involve the wrath of creation itself. Thus, the Nagas use common symbols of authority such as the decorated spears, the kind that is not normally used in war[5]. Among the Nagas, the mithun, buffalo, hornbill, pig, dog, cock and lesser creatures of the earth and sky are accorded their rightful place in the social structure in descending order of importance. They are symbols of considerable ritual significance[6].

It is an accepted fact that there are a number of indigenous tribal people in North-East India, who are called "Tribals" or "Tribes", each having its own culture and history. In Manipur, there are different communities in which the major groups are Meities, Meitei-Pangan (Meitei Muslim), hill or tribal people (such as Nagas, Kuki-Chin etc). There are other minor communities also. The tribals have their own highly evolved system of administration. Each village in the case of the Nagas is like a republic. Linguistically, they belong to the Tibeto-Burman family. Despite having similar roots, their languages are not intelligible to each other, especially, among the Naga groups. Almost 80% of the hill tribes are Christians. The process began from the late 19th century.

There are some similarities between the cultures of the Israelites and the tribal people of Manipur especially the 'Zo' (Chin-Kuki-Mizo) group. This similarity as a result makes them believe that they are originally from Israel the Promised Land. In 1974, the word 'MIZO' was translated into Mizoram Israel Zionist Organisation (MIZO). They believe that the word Pathian (a word for God among 'Zo') was derived from the English word 'Python', 'Jesu' (Jesus) from Zeu soters (Zeu the Saviour), 'Christ' from a Sanskrit word 'Kris'[7] in many tribal religions of the olden days, there are certain rites of purification. After a man's death, the wife and the family members are still living with the spirit of the deceased one until and unless they perform the purification ceremony. However, with the coming of Christianity in the late 19th Century, the old beliefs, customs and traditions of the tribals were turned upside down.[7]

It is not possible to trace the history of the coming of Christianity tribe-wise. With the advent of the British rule in the beginning of the 19th Century, the tribals were exposed to Christianity and significant numbers embraced it. Conversion of a people into a new major religion always produces basic changes in the social and cultural life of the people concerned. In a tribal society, there is a close tie between the religious, cultural, social and political institutions. Culture itself has many definitions: According to Krocbee and Kluckhohm, "Culture is learned; that is greatly variable, that is manifested in institutions, thought patterns and material objects." E. B. Taylor described it as, "that complex whole which include knowledge, belief, art, moral, law, custom and any other capabilities and habits acquired by man as a member of a society"[8] Culture is the way in which a group of people live, think, feel, organize themselves, celebrate and share life. In every culture, there are underlying system of values, meanings and views of the world that are expressed visibly in languages, gestures, symbols, rituals and styles[9]. Culture is also what a social group considers as the best and sum- total of its thinking, living and expressing.

Religion intertwines itself with culture by way of giving shape in a concrete belief in the Supreme. Through the cultural expressions, it reaches out to the beyond. God becomes someone who gives meaning to the existence of a particular group of people.[10]. The value system of the tribes and sub-tribes of the North-East are essentially reflected, as in a mirror, in the Hynniewtreps value system. At the first Divine Durbar in Heaven, the Momentous decision was taken, to sent the Hynniewtreps to the world for a definite purpose-to rule, to govern, to administer according to the maxims "Ka Ni a, Kaba Tam" i.e. reason, discussion and consensus. The value system of a people is the real source of its world view viz., its relationship with God, with the human race as a whole, and with the universe at large.[11] Some of the most important elements of the tribal concept of themselves, in consequence of their value system are

(a) They are a sovereign people with a definite purpose, and a role to play in history as rulers and administrators, (b) They are a people whose individuals are all equal, (c) They are a people who believe that all their individual members have the same rights and duties as human beings. This sense of inborn human dignity, certainty and security of confidence and enthusiasm, became a reality in their body politic, in their social and economic life. Their mode of ruling and governing was democratic; social and judicial justice triumphed. The simple agricultural economic system was sound, all were practically self-sufficient, borders were safe and well-defended, and theft was practically unknown. The life of the tribes and sub-tribes of the North-East was truly human- thanks to their value system, [12] besides believing in an essentially benevolent God, they also believed in the existence of numerous spirits who were either good or evil. The evil spirits were ill disposed towards evil beings. These evil spirits which were hostile to man, had to be appeased to ward off misfortune, sickness, and death by sacrifice of animals such as cock, dog, pig, etc. They were propitiated by sacrifices that were offered by the village authority or the chief. The good spirits were worshipped through sacrifices for bestowal of blessings, prosperity, and fecundity etc.[13]

The Nagas in general believe in the existence of plurality of gods-Supreme God, gods of various natural elements, evil spirits, village deities, forest deities, god of the land, of the dead, etc. The Supreme God, called 'Oramai' by the Maos, 'Kameo'/'Varivara' by the Tangkhuls, 'Raguang' by the Zeliangrong, lives somewhere above the sky and the place is called 'Tingkaokai'.[14] The Kukis-Chin-Mizo believe in the existence of a Supreme-Being or God, Pathen/Pathian/Pasian. They also believe that there were forces alive in the nature of spirit, which were hostile to man and had the power to harm people by way of sickness. In order to ward off misfortune, sickness, by the spirits, or sometimes to appease them, they performed certain rite and sacrifices for the well being of their lives and properties. They believed, that naturals objects such as mountains, caves, rivers, trees, stones and especially 'Siih'-a place where Kukis believe, bad spirits dwelt, are the abode of all these Thilhas/siha (evil/bad spirits). Apart from offering sacrificial ritual to the Thilhas (spirits), the Kukis also kept Indoi (house god/family deity) in the house.

Inn-doi/Indawi or Doi-bom is the house god or deity of the Kukis. Each house-holder has family Inn-doi. It serves the whole family so long as the members all live in one house. There is no fixed time for making the Inn-doi, and it is usually done when a separate household feels that they suffered from lack of health or of wealth. In making a new inn-doi, the Thempu /Siampu (Priest) play an important part. And for making Inn-doi, the following things are to be collected.

1. Vohpi-lu (a female pig-skull).
2. Kelki (horns of a he-goat).
3. Khaokol (bamboo bangle) 7 round each (double)
4. Peng/um (small gourd) 2 pieces, one for 'Zu' and the other for seeds (one each of the round type).
5. Tengdop/Teipi (spear)
6. Chemkol (Dao).
7. Belval (a circular stand for a jar made of bamboo split- differs from clan to clan).

These items are bound together with a creeper, called 'Khaopi', 'Khaokol' is a ring-like cord made of bamboo, called 'Gopi', peeled and thinned, called 'Gopi-naang' are used for binding together the spear and the dao with seven rounds on each side in a bangle-shaped fashion. Likewise, the gourd is used for two purposes-one as a container of 'Zu' and the other as a container of the seeds. The above mentioned ingredients tied together are called 'Indawi'. These are bound together and placed at the inner portion of the roof of the portico, called 'Hongcha'. This is the place where the rice pounder called 'Sum' is placed and the poultry of the family called 'Ahgil' is constructed. The portion of the house where 'Indawi' is kept is called 'Bichiing'.[15]

The tribal society is basically a service oriented society. The main features of their social organization are: the village system, the institution of chieftainship/headman, the council of elders, and the youth organization, concretized in the institution of the bachelor's dormitory. But there is a tendency, sometimes to dismiss tribal religion as single animism. In his book "The Aboriginal Tribes of India," Stephen Fuchs referring to the tribes of the North-East writes: Most tribes believe in one deity, superior to the rest, a strong belief in the existence of a supreme being. He adds, "Christianity is a very community-oriented religion-very much in harmony with tribal outlook and mentality in general. Christianity is also equally a religion of personal discipleship and loyalty to Christ, to the extent of forging family ties, bonds of tribe and clan, for the sake of Christ and his values." This is evident in the celebration of 'Feast of Merit' of the Nagas and 'Chon/Ton' (celebration) of the Kukis-Chins. It is a feast in which "richer persons of the society share their abundance with others". It was a sign of thanksgiving to God for their wealth as well as to show equality and oneness with others, notwithstanding their riches. It is where the rich is 'subjected to the requirements of social relationships. The value implied in the sharing of one's wealth is a conspicuous gospel value, as shown in the call of Jesus to the young man 'to sell all what you have and give to the poor (Mk 10:23-27) and whoever wants to be first must be the slave of all (Mk10-34-45) God's sharing of his riches with humanity by sending his Son to be born as a human being could not be better commemorated by the Nagas than in the feast of merit. Hence, Christmas for a nagaized Christianity could be the feast of merit and this could be celebrated annually.[16]

Amongst tribal people with any connection to Christianity, many questions arise in relation to their culture. For the most part of the one hundred years of Christian mission to tribal people, virtually all aspects of 'native' culture were condemned as 'primitive' or even 'demonic' or 'satanic'. There was an insensitive conflation of culture and religion in the minds of the early missionaries. But in our understanding, culture is primarily produced by the creative impulse in the nature of human-kind[17]. Tribal cultures will certainly, not adapt out of necessity because of the important part played by value concepts in the determination of cultural patterns. There is a close affinity between morality and culture[18]. This means that theology must concern itself with the culture of the people. The point here is that, it takes a lot to translate this seemingly "heathen" cosmology into a Christian format.

The emergence of a western world's colonizing system in the 15th century revived legal speculations on the rights and status of the non-Christian people that Europeans wanted to subjugate. The missionaries often depicted in literature as having more concern than the British colonial authorities have for the indigenous people as far as "Civilizing Mission" was concerned. The missionaries could, without hesitation, root out what they thought to be archaic traditional customs. It was a different story for the British, who traumatized by the cataclysm that engulfed Europe during the First World War, were concerned with retaining and bringing order in their colonies. This prompted the British to accord to traditional bodies their rightful place or to invent a superstructure wherever appropriate traditional structures were not readily present. It was a restraining force for the relentless missionary enterprise of cultural engineering. Nonetheless, their collective role during the colonial era undoubtedly formed a composite "colonizing agency". This implied the control of a people, their education and literature and polity formation.

Edmund Leach, the practitioner of structuralism among social anthropologists, described – "The great surge of 19th century Christian missionary endeavor was diverted towards the primitives. In the eyes of the administration the Christian conversion of a Buddhist or a Muslim might entail all sorts of unforeseeable political consequences, but surely the conversion of a cannibal or a head-hunter could only be for the good". The well-financed schools of the Christian missions often provided an education vastly superior to anything contained in the traditional system of the "civilized majority".

One of the ways in which imperial nations used to subjugate colonies and their indigenous inhabitants was by means of religion. The colonial situation introduced institutions to assume new functions. Pax Britannica brought in its wake, the American Baptist Mission. It initiated disruption of traditional culture and imposition of western beliefs and values on indigenous customs and rituals. Normally, when cultures are altered and redefined, people lose a sense of the way life used to be. In other parts of the globe, the colonial force and missionary zeal succeeded in dislodging traditional culture and people from their history and ancestry. Missionaries and the schools they set up in indigenous communities implemented this policy. Indeed, indigenous peoples in many parts of the world identify education as a crucial factor in the historical process of their marginalization. This resulted in the virtual obliteration of most of the indigenous peoples' way of life- their cultural practices, traditions, arts and languages. This kind of process, however, did not entirely overwhelm the Nagas. One reason could be that the British magistracy and Christian missionaries were constantly at loggerheads with each other. As of now, Christianity remains a central principle of faith and a crucial element of Naga solidarity.

After the advent of British colonialism, tribals of Manipur started embracing Christianity preached by missionaries coming from the west as for instance Pettigrew of Arthington Mission and Watkin Roberts of the Welsh Calvinistic Methodist Foreign Mission Society (WCFMS).[19] In spite of resistance by the traditional chiefs and their close followers in the initial period, Christianity became the religion of the whole community (tribals) within fifty years of mission work. There had been a total rearrangement in the structure of the system of beliefs and practices. The old belief in the evil spirits and the world of evil spirits dominating the human world was gone. However, it was precisely on this system of beliefs and practices that the traditional values became manifested and agricultural work gained its rightful place in maintaining the village solidarity. The traditional base of solidarity was now upset by the conversion to the Christianity and a social revolution was in offing.

While the traditional society was unable to accommodate the common man to acquire agricultural wealth, the new structure, with commercialization process in operation was relatively elastic.[20] Prof B. Pakem expressed that 'as the new process of Christianization in the society of North East India is concerned; the ready acceptance of Christianity was because of their feelings of deprivation. Christianity was in fact, not welcomed in the beginning particularly by the traditional elite, for they thought that it was depriving them of their traditional privileges such as the use of rice beer and their traditional power.

Tracing the origin of Christianity, we find that it was the American Baptist Mission in Burma, which made the first attempt to establish its Mission station in Manipur, an erstwhile princely state, as early as 1836. But this was not possible because of the opposition from the local native government which had accepted Vaishnavite Hinduism as a principal religion by royal edict in 1705. With it, orthodoxy and conservatism became entrenched among the native aristocrats who tended to look upon every movement of the white people with misgivings and suspicion. In complete disregard of their sentiment, James Johnston the Political Agent of Manipur made every arrangement for any Missionary who would be willing to work among the people of the state.[21]

The Tribals lived in isolation for there was no inter-village connectivity, there were merely a few bridle paths criss crossing the hills. As such, they were untouched by the 'advanced' or 'material' cultures of other people around them. They had their own cultures – a symbolic system that they construct to make their community and world, life and history meaningful.[22]

But with the coming of Christianity and colonialism, tribal society began to undergo a period of transition and a cataclysmic upheaval. From a primitive society that used to subsist on shifting cultivation, it was catapulted forward, to grapple with modern ideas, technologies and way of life. The transition was explosive not gradual. There was common ownership of land, forests, rivers, mountains etc. Every aspect of tribal life is in terms of intense mutual interaction. In this, also lies the basic orientation of the tribal society, sharing with each other what they have and helping to bear each other's burdens, like the first Christian communities, seen in the pages of the Acts of the Apostles.[23]

The Christian Church has been able to establish itself in Manipur right from the outset; it began to look for members of the local community who could be trained to lead and man the entire church – its institutions, its services and its hierarchy itself. For instance, local Catholic priests and nuns have their roots both in Christianity and in their own culture. Thus, they are simultaneously a testimony that the church remains rooted in the faith and in the local church.[24] The primary mission of the church is the proclamation of Christ's message and when the missionaries first came to Manipur, they found the people of the hills (tribals) open to this message. They aimed at an all-round formation, primarily through education, building people to become the greatest glory of God.[25]

Despite ushering in modernity of thought, behavior, beliefs, lifestyle, the Church of Christ existed for mission. The acceptance of Christianity was partly because of the consciousness of the missionaries that the service of faith of which promotion of justice is an absolute requirement should be seen in its cultural context. This was reinforced with an integral evangelization and a preferential option for the poor. The Church teaches to discern in what we experience within ourselves and around us the presence of the Lord who 'works and labours with us in our cultures in His incarnation' and has called each one of us to collaborate in His ongoing Paschal work.[26]

Christianity in Manipur is so much indebted to Mr. William Pettigrew who came to Assam under the auspices of the Arthington Mission in 1891.[27] Rev. William Pettigrew who came as a missionary under the Arthington Aboriginese Mission but later became a Baptist, arrived in Imphal, the capital of Manipur on the 6th January 1894.

Rev. William Pettigrew, an Englishman was born in Edinburg, Scotland on 5th January, 1869. He was educated in Livingstone College, London. He was at first a member of the Anglican Church. Later he was convinced of the inadequacy of

Infant Baptism and, therefore, accepted Believers Baptism while he was in Dhaka, working as a missionary under Arthington Aboriginese Mission. He remained an Anglican and worked under the same mission till he joined the Baptist Church at Sibsagar in 1896. After he joined the Baptist Mission, he was called and ordained to the Gospel Ministry. The same year in November 13, he was married to Alice Gorehome of Bringhton, England.[28]

Rev. William Pettigrew, after his arrival in Imphal established a Lower Primary School at Thangmeiband.[29] Pettigrew began to think that his call was among the Meiteis and was anxious to preach the Gospel among them. But the Hinduised Meiteis construed Pettigrew's preaching as a deliberate attempt to impose upon them the government's religion.[30] Maxwell, the then Political Agent on his return from Furlong, took an alarming view and expressed his fear that the trouble might arise if Pettigrew's activities were not nipped in the bud because the Meiteis held on to the tenets of the Hindu religion almost to fanaticism.[31]

Pettigrew was sadly disappointed because the door for missionary work in Manipur was closed. Maxwell came to his rescue and suggested that he should work in the hill areas – the north-east area at Ukhrul among the Tangkhul Nagas.[32] It is said that he (Pettigrew) first approached a Thado-Kuki chief, Kamkholun Singson of Senvon village for permission to locate his work there in 1896. When permission was denied he went to the Tangkhul area.[33] However, this story of his visit to Senvon is a matter of dispute. In 1909, one copy of St. John's Gospel in Lushai dialect distributed by the missionaries in the Lushai hills found its way to the hand of Mr. Kamkholun, chief of Senvon. This time he invited the missionaries from Aizawl to come and tell him and his people about the Gospel.[34] It is also said that he went and meet Sanikapani a government. Interpreter, a Mao

Naga and tried to purchase some land in Mao area. Sanikapani told Pettigrew that without the consent of village authorities he could not sell any land. So, then sixteen village headmen were called for consultation. Not only was Mr. Pettigrew's request for purchasing land for religious work turned down, but also he was warned by the village authorities not to remain in their area any longer.[35]

In his search for a new location for his work, Pettigrew visited Paoyi, Shiroi, Khangkhul and Ukhrul. At Ukhrul Pettigrew established a temporary building and the villagers were invited to learn to read. However, the response of the villagers was not affirmative. As a result, Maj. Maxwell, Manipur Political Agent requested the village elders to send their wards to the school.

In an effort to establish Christianity on a firm footing, Pettigrew realized that dialogue was essential and so he took the trouble of learning and mastering the Tangkhul dialect. He produced a Tangkhul grammar and so he took the first step in putting down Tangkhul dialect in written form. This was a milestone in the process of modernization of the tribals, the Tangkhuls in particular, for it facilitated, dialogue, communication, exchange of ideas, communication understanding which received an impetus from subsequent publiccations, which both informed and taught. Not that his work was not riddled with difficulties. (Earlier reliance was only on Oral Tradition) Out of the 20 students that attended Pettigrew School 12 of them were soon won over to Christ in 1901. The school continued to grow and between 1896 and 1905, the progress was conspicuous. In 1902, Pettigrew succeeded in establishing the first Church in Ukhrul.[36] By 1907, the Christians numbered seventy.[37]

Meanwhile the State government appointed Pettigrew as Superintendent of the first real census of the hill tribes (1910-

11) because the missionary was the only man who knew the language of the hill tribes. The census work definitely enabled the missionary and his native workers to explore more areas hitherto unvisited.[38] In 1911, he obtained permission to go to the southwest of Manipur. There with the help of the Kom students, Tiba and Longkhubel Kilong, Pettigrew preached the Gospel in the villages of Khongjang, Parbung, Lailong, Songsang, Pherzawl and others.[39]

The arrival of U. M. Fox in Ukhrul in 1911 was a great relief for Pettigrew as the need for more missionaries arose. During the first five years of his stay, Rev. Fox opened the door to higher education. In 1915, Rev. U. M. Fox baptized Maipak Kabui, Kachindai Kacha Naga, Bhagirath Gurkha, Thanga Hmar, Jaison Kom and Manjaching at Imphal. Longkhubel Kilong was appointed as the first evangelist among the Kukis and the Koms. Through his endeavour, the Longkhong Church was established. The Magui Church, which is the oldest, came into existence through Nehseh, the first convert among the Thadou Kukis.[40] Added to all this, due to Pettigrew's efforts, by 1917, there were 355 church members in five different groups in various parts of the State.[41]

After 22 years of his stay in Ukhrul Pettigrew shifted his mission stations/Headquarters to Kangpokpi after obtaining permission from the Maharaja of Manipur. With the consent of the Maharaja on 7th November, 1919 a Dispensary and Lepers Asylum was established there. Perhaps emulating Pettigrew, the American Baptist Mission established an Orphanage at Kangpokpi M. E. School and since then Kangpokpi became the Mission Headquarters, with Pettigrew taking charge of the Schools and Dr. Crozier who arrived from Tura, Garo hills took responsibility for the dispensary, the Leper Asylum and the north-west area.[42]

The Kangpokpi Mission School was established and Mr. Miksha Shimray, the first graduate of the Ukhrul Mission School was appointed the Headmaster. In 1920, the administration of the hills was separated from the plains. For more effective work of administration, the hill areas was divided into three sub-divisions, namely, Ukhrul, Churachandpur and Tamenglong.

The growth of new local Churches were now more rapid in the Ukhrul sub-division. Correspondingly, it became difficult to supervise them. In 1920, the Mission work in the Ukhrul sub-division was divided into three field-circles; the western, northern and eastern circles. There was no southern circle as no local Churches were organized yet in that area. Three Superintendent Pastors were appointed and assigned for each circle.[43]

In order to consolidate the groups of believers scattered all over the territory, it was decided to appoint head evangelists of the several areas that had been opened up for evangelical work. They had to submit monthly reports of their works of caring for the scattered Christian communities and evangelizing the non-Christians. A Kom Kuki was appointed for the southern part of the State, a Thadou Kuki for the western areas, and a Tangkhul Naga for northern and eastern section of the State. This arrangement continued to the time of the great revival, 1923-1924. In May 1921, a revival began among the Tangkhul Nagas, led by two young men, one the headmaster of the school at Ukhrul, Miksha Shimrei. In 1923, there were 1018, who took Baptism. By 1925, all the Churches and village schools had become self-supporting, Church pastors and teachers were paid by Church and Association funds.[44]

Meanwhile the first evangelist among the Kukis was one Mr. Ngulhao Thomsong. He worked among the Kukis and Anals. His work bore fruit and that led to the organization of a local

Church in Tujang Waichong village in 1916. After his return from the war, (as a volunteer to France in world war1) he entered Government service for two years but left the service to continue with evangelism among Anals. In three years of work, about 334 Anals and Kukis were converted in southern Manipur. Another Kuki evangelist whose personal efforts brought reconciliation between the Kukis and the Rongmei Nagas was Paokho Sitlhou. This Kuki man learnt the Rongmei dialect and translated hymns and some scriptures into the Rongmei dialect. Paokho Sitlhou married a Rongmei woman and through his efforts and influence, the ill feelings among the two tribes were considerably minimized and relationship improved. A major tribe in Manipur is Mao, which is also called 'quasi-Angami' being akin to the Eastern Angami Nagas of Nagaland. The Maos were conservative in outlook and extremely superstitious. Converting such conservative Maos was an uphill task for the evangelists. Later, several young Maos from Punanamei and Pudunamei villages went to study at the Somdal village school in Ukhrul where they were converted. On their return home, they evangelized among the Maos. The early evangelists in Mao area faced a series of hardships and oppositions from local population. But as a result of their untiring effort a local Church was formally organized at Mao Gate in 1927.[45]

The beginning of the mission enterprise in the southern Manipur is very much related to the revival in Wales, England. The revival was led by Evan. Roberts around 1904-1906 with around 34,000 persons converting to the Christian faith. Watkins R. Roberts was one of those who experienced a turning point in his career. He zealously devoted most of his spare time to reading the scriptures and writings of great biblical scholars. After, reading through Reuben. A. Torrey and Charles Spurgeon's sermons and their writings it touched his soul and doubts rose in his mind. Roberts then made a solemn decision to proclaim the victory of Calvary amongst the tribesmen in North-East India. Watkin R. Roberts was born on September, 1886 at Carvaervon, North Wales and breathed his last at his home town in Toronto in April 20, 1969.[46]

The implanting of the Gospel in the South District and Watkin R. Roberts are inseparable. It was Watkins R. Roberts who, accompanying Dr. Peter Fraser to Lushai Hills in December 1908, first broke the silence of the claimed but untraded southern Manipur hills in 1910 for undenominational mission field. On October 14, 1908, W. Roberts sailed for India along with Dr. and Mrs. Peter Fraser who were sent by the Welsh Missionary Society. W. Roberts was an independent missionary travelling via Calcutta. In the Lushai hills, Dr. Fraser opened a medical clinic, Robert was his assistant, and Robert then learnt the Lushai language. One day, some young men having a slightly different outlook came to the clinic. These young men were from southern Manipur, looking for education and sponsorship to continue their education in Aizawl. They were Lungpau from Maite Village and Thangkai from Bualtang Village, Churachandpur. Robert's heart was greatly touched and he wanted to give them something so that they could learn about the Gospel.

Prior to all this, the Calvanist Methodist church of the Welsh Mission had sent Rev. Savidge and J. H. Lorrain who had reached Aizawl in 1884. These two missionaries after working for 4 years translated the 'Gospel of St. John' and the 'Acts of the Apostles' in Lushai[47]. Robert in 1909 received 15 pounds from Emily Davies, Hamstead, England to meet his personal requirements. Robert instead of using the money to meet his needs brought one hundred and four copies of St. John's Gospel in Lushai dialect and distributed the copies to different hill chiefs and persons who came to the mission's clinic at Aizawl. He also enclosed R. Dala's (from whom Roberts learnt Lushai dialect). "The Way to Salvation" with the copy, one of the copies fell in the hands of the Senvon Chief, Kamkholun Singson who once denied permission to Pettigrew to preach in his area now he was deeply moved by the Gospel and invited Roberts to his village. So Watkin R. Roberts took two young men with him and marched towards Senvon. The two young men were Lungpau and Thangkai. They reached Senvon village in February 5, 1910. It was a long and hazardous journey of 5 days walk from Aizawl. Thus, W. R. Roberts as requested by the Chief started the work of preaching the Gospel in Senvon village.

Thangkai was born in 1881 in Sialkawt, Mizoram. He was the only son of Awnzala and Tawngai. Thangkai's parents moved to Maite in Manipur from Mizoram. Unfortunate death came to Thangkai's parents. Thangkai with his sister Khawlngai were helpless and could not afford to make a living, so they moved to Bualtang hoping to get a helping hand from their relatives in making a livelihood.

Lungpau was born in 1882 in the Chin Hills (Burma). He had two brothers and three sisters. Unlike Thangkai, Lungpau came from a wealthy family. They moved to Maite village from Thungcham village, the oldest village of the Vaiphei and are also considered as the roof of the Vaiphei in the southern district of Manipur.[48]

In 1907, a great famine struck the southern district of Manipur. Thangkai and Lungpau went to Sinzawl with some British Officials to distribute aid and a supply of rice. Here they saw for the first time paper work, associated with the task, they were taken aback, but resolved to learn, to read and write. In 1908, they started learning the beginner lessons in Sairang and later on at Phuaibung.[49]

Thangkai and Lungpau now under the guidance of Watkins R. Roberts decided to move to the southern district of Manipur, which was still virgin territory. Westernization was unknown to this area as also the Gospel. W. R. Roberts was very anxious to visit the area and commence his preaching of the Gospel. Roberts chose Thangkai and Lungpau to go with him to Manipur as both of them were from that area. In their sojourn, Roberts and his assistants passed through Zokhosang, Sifa, Dailo and finally reached the border of Manipur and Mizoram. They continued their journey to Parvachawm. By the time they reached southern Manipur, every villager welcomed them and moreover everyone was surprised to see a person with a different color, dress etc. Thangkai and Lungpau were 'born again' and accepted the faith of Christianity on 17th Feb, 1910 in Vervek village. W. R. Roberts claims that two of them were the first fruits of his missionary activity in the whole southern district of Manipur. Later on, Thangkai and Lungpau were baptized by W. R. Roberts.[50]

On May 7, 1910, W. R. Roberts, Thangkai and Lungpau returned and reached Senvon village. On 18th May 1910, Roberts with his two new converts reached Aizawl and apprised Dr. Fraser and his wife about the mission to Manipur. Thangkai began his evangelistic work and proceeded to Leisen village. Up to 1914, more than 200 people were converted to Christianity. In 1911, he worked as a teacher in his own village, Bualtang. When W. R. Roberts was about to leave Senvon, the Chief requested him to establish a school there. In Aizawl, Roberts extended an invitation for volunteers who would work as evangelist teachers at Senvon. Three bible students viz., Savawma, Vanzika and Thangchingpuia offered their service and arrived at Senvon on May 7, 1910. The first mission school at Senvon was now established. Thangur, Thangneirum and Kaithang became the first converts through their mission school.

To establish the mission work at Senvon, Roberts sent for Rev. R. Dala and Taisena. Roberts then visited Imphal to inform the Political Agent about the development in the Senvon area. However, the Political Agent refused to grant permission to W. R. Roberts to open another mission in Manipur. The Political Agent anticipated that the presence of another Christian center beside that of the Baptist mission might jeopardize the situation. W. R. Roberts was warned to leave the state, which he refused to do. Roberts continued and his mission expanded which in course of time led to crossing the boundary between the Indo- Burma Thadou Kuki Pioneer Mission and Baptist Mission. By the year 1912, the Christian ministries were able to employ the real natives of Manipur, namely Thangkai and Lungpau and Awmtea as teacher evangelists with a pay of ₹ 6 per month.[51]

The Baptist Church was the first mission to enter Manipur state; but later on, other Church missions too appeared to share in the work of evangelization of the tribes. The success of the large scale conversion; particularly after the World War-1, was due to the efforts of various Christian missions, viz., the American Baptist, the North-East India General Mission, the Seventh Day Adventist, Independent Church of India, The evangelical Free Church of India, etc.[52]

According to the Census figures of Manipur

Year	*Population*	*Percentage of Christian Population*
1971	10, 72,753	26.03
1981	14, 20,953	29.60
1991	18, 26,714	30.00 (not exact figures)
2001	23, 88,634	39.00

Although the mission centre was in the hill area of Manipur, Pettigrew did not neglect the evangelistic work in the plain area. He tried to win the plain people to Christ as well. Thus, early in

1916 a Church, the Second Baptist Church in Manipur was organized by Pettigrew at Keishamthong in Imphal town with 18 church members composed of a Gorkha, Sema, Meiteis, Rongmeis and Kukis. In 1920, five Christian families moved to Thangmeiband in the North of Imphal, settling on a plot of land given by the government for this purpose in appreciation of the service rendered by the mission and many Christians during the First World War.[53] At the time of Japanese invasion, the site was abandoned and reverted to the Government. However, in 1956, at the request of the Manipur Baptist Convention, it was once again made available for Christian use. The MBC is now located in this land.[54] Though very little progress was made in Manipur during the first twenty years of Christian work good foundations had been laid for the rapid growth of the church which followed the First World War.

The advent of Christianity into Manipur marks the beginning of a new life and its introduction into the hills is pregnant with many effects of far reaching importance. The hill people, though ignorant as they were, hardly believed that the new religion would work miracles among them. But it brought civilization to those head hunting people who enthralled themselves with blood feuds between different villages, setting one clan against another in relentless feuding. No one would deny the name 'Savage' for our people, when our forefathers were naked and their knowledge limited, when they were fighting each other for no lasting benefit and when life and property were in secure. We should feel proud that we have come from that stage to the present civilized state. "The dark is gone and we are now in contact with the outside world."[55]

Leaving the old days behind, people have now become more amiable, tolerant and understanding. There is a yearning for peace, brotherhood and love. K. P. Guite writes, "Had not Christianity been introduced in the hill areas of Manipur, the conditions of the tribal would be very much otherwise and would be all the more an uphill and colossal task for their development." But now, owing to the impact of Christianity on their life, many of them being enlightened to the unfailing teaching of the Lord Jesus Christ with the vehement forces of teachings found in their bible, the tribal have been virtually transformed traditionally, culturally, socially, educationally, economically and religiously.[56]

The Christian Missionary Movement had initially evoked opposition and persecution followed. Missionaries were often beaten up, chased by villagers and in some cases, they were not even permitted to enter the villages. However, once the gospel message spread far and wide, hundreds of people who heard the truth of the new gospel fell under the power of God and embraced Christianity. Hence, it can be described as the greatest significant force, which has given birth to a new age, by the subsequent transformation of a savage into a fairly sober and rational being.[57]

The worth of the missionary is acknowledged in almost all places, all over the world. It was Sir Hector Duff who after a great many years of administration in Africa, found it impossible to condemn missionary enterprise, in spite of much harm that it caused, because it induced so much that was clearly for the good of the people.[58] The Maharaja of Manipur permitted Christian missionaries subject to the condition that no preaching was to be undertaken among the Meitei population. But the missionaries had at least the freedom to approach the hill people with all openness. In the last hundred years or so, the missionaries have done a yeoman's service for the social political and economic uplift of the people. It is also an acknowledged fact that a society does not possess that inertia or the potential to change by itself. An external element, a force, an individual, a religion have been factors responsible for change of all types. That is why many scholars overwhelmingly rate the impact of Missionary Endeavour as one of the main agents of cultural, political, social and economic change brought about in Manipur.

Along with many other forces of change, the impact of Christianity in North- East India has brought about the drastic changes in the lifestyles of those who have embraced the religion. Sachidanand adds that all over the world, the church has been one of the most important agencies of social change.[59] Tarun Goswami claims that Christianity has not eliminated the tribals from their traditional and cultural milieu. It has not disturbed the inbuilt framework of their ancient culture, lore and lifestyle. Rather it is Christianity that has been suitably modified, may not though be in its basic tenets, but definitely in its outward forms and practices, under the strong and perpetual impact of a human culture handed down the ages. As such, their ancients are still remembered, revered and obeyed.[60]

From 1924 onwards, it became apparent that a kind of intellectual awakening had occurred among the tribal Christians. They clad themselves in the new garments of revolutionary thoughts and ideas, and emphasised Gospel values. Christianity, which initially was looked upon as foreign was now embraced whole-heartedly. Among the organized religions, Christianity boasts of a well-structured organization, with a papal history from apostolic times, and a strong tradition to standby. It prides itself as a religion that has a history of its own, a history that is verifiable, rational and empirical.[61]

With Christianity came education and education brought forth the very identity and prevailing cultural traits. As Horam writes, "In the quest for Identity, the Tangkhuls are in the process of questioning, revaluing, readapting, and if need be disregarding the age-old ways of life."[62]

The coming of Christianity and modernization has brought a great transformation in the socio-cultural life of the hill tribes of Manipur.[63] Their standard of life in those days was indeed abysmally low. Their houses and even those built inside the village compound were dirty. They kept all domestic animals like buffaloes, cows, mithuns, pigs, dogs and chickens in the same house where they lived. Now Christianity taught them essentials of hygiene and healthy living, the importance of separate spaces for humans and animals. The impact of Christianity also felt in the field of improving the quality of life of people- a relatively modern concept. It was common for the tribals to live in the same house as their animals who were a source of wealth and prestige. The simple, uneducated tribal was not conversant with the nuances of good or healthy living, and their habitations generally represented the minimum that an individual needs to protect him from hunger, want, inclement weather. Moreover, water was not easily available on hill-tops where tribals settled for politic and strategic reasons. The tribals had no money to spend on luxuries, as a result, their surroundings were generally unhealthy and unhygienic, a breeding ground for disease. The missionaries taught the simple tribal the importance of keeping the body clean, taught them all essentials of personal hygiene especially Mrs. Pettigrew, and keeping their homes and surroundings clean and tidy. This in turn led to an improvement in health and not only of the individuals but also their domestic animals, for the missionaries brought with them advanced ideas of how to increase agricultural productivity both in their kitchen gardens and cultivated paddy fields. The missionaries also introduced them to the concept of nutrition and a balanced diet. Although the missionaries preached against the abuse of alcohol, they were not completely successful in eradicating the excesses associated with drinking rice beer and wine. But in some places the 'ZU' (rice beer) was replaced by tea, and the missionaries advocated limiting alcoholic intake. Simultaneously they emphasized the necessity of co-operation and participation in community meals and festivals.

Not only was worship of One God a spiritual solace to the tribals, but giving up of animal sacrifices to the spirits had a decided economic advantage, as the incidence of sacrifice bore heavily on the poor and marginalized. And the majority of the tribals at the time of the advent of Christianity were poor farmers, although a certain percentage had achieved self-sufficiency in production. The Christian missionaries completely won the hearts of the tribal people and as a result they were maligned in certain quarters. However, they especially the Catholic missionaries were praised and defended in the Indian Parliament by the then Prime Minister of India, Mr. Nehru himself "We have proofs that there is nothing anti-social and nothing objectionable in their conduct. You also go and do what the Catholic missionaries do, and win over the tribals if you can".[64] Moreover the missionaries established centres- Churches, schools, dispensaries in the under-developed regions of the state, exercising in practice their option for the poor, thus bringing even the poorest to the threshold of modernisation.

The missionaries helped the tribals to come into their own. Prior to their advent they lived on the margins deprived of roads, electricity, healthcare, drinking water, suffering from in accessibility and deprivation of all kinds, for instance if a tribal villager felt ill he had to be carried on a bamboo stretcher for long distances by relatives on foot. But with the impact of Christianity and modernisation, the missionaries introduced modern concept of medicine, they also established dispensaries, clinics and hospitals and provided state of the art facilities to even the poorest tribal Christians. This is apparent in the services of institutions like the Catholic Medical Centre at

Imphal, staffed and manned by specialists in the fields, the Leisiphung Christian hospital in Ukhrul, the Sielmat Christian hospital in Churachandpur and the Kangpokpi Christian hospital at Kangpokpi. They charge nominal fees to the poor Christians and even provide free medicines and food packages to the poor and needy. Moreover, the hospitals have inspired many tribal Christians to study medicine and become doctors in their own right, adding to the numbers of the middle class in tribal society. Provision of timely and proper medical care has improved the overall-health status of the tribals and enhanced their life span. It is common to find senior citizens among the tribals healthy, active and productive.

The missionaries taught simple remedies for ailments like common cold, cough, fever, diarrohea etc. They taught the concept of holistic health, mind and body; they also created awareness of social issues and afforded advice and counsel to all who sought it. In course of time they arranged orientation courses for young people, those intending to marry, seniors and elders, marginalized etc. They gave special attention to the Sacrament of marriage and almost put a stop to the practice of elopement which was prevalent among the tribals and which won social acceptance.

Dr. and Mrs. Crozier, the American Baptist Foreign Mission Society Missionaries had taken the lead in establishing a leper's home (asylum) at Kangpokpi in 1921. Leprosy at the time of the coming of the missionaries was regarded both a curse and dreaded disease. The missionaries introduced modern methods of treating the disease. At first, Dr. Crozier made a plea for opening a Leper asylum to the State Government, but the government plainly refused the plea on the ground of financial constraints. But the Darbar advised the American Baptist Mission to look after the lepers and to retain the lepers under Dr. Crozier's care in their asylum. The State also made an assurance to make a contribution towards the cost of maintaining the lepers in Manipur. By 1930-31, there were 130 patients, of which 83 were Christians and 47 non-Christians. There were 32 new admissions during the year. Sixteen lepers were discharged as cured, 8 died and 14 rans away before completion of the treatment. The State contributed a grant-in-aid of ₹3,000/- per annum towards its upkeep and the remainder of the money came from Mission Funds. The total cost of the colony during the year amounted to ₹4738/-. They also enthused the tribal not to shun and discriminate against lepers. Their actions were regarded as revolutionary, as at the time, no person wanted to associate let alone help a leper.

As the Gospel message spread, tribals envisaged a new society and a new creation 'everyone will be filled with Christ and Christ will be all in all (Col. 3:11). But to fully understand the Gospel message, education was regarded as a pre-requisite.' The Missionaries, especially the first entrants and later the Catholic Fathers and Sisters believed "Since everyman of whatever dignity of a person, has an inalienable right to education corresponding to his proper destiny, and suited to his native talents, his sex, his cultural background and his ancestral heritage. At the same time, this education should pave the way to brotherly association with other people, so that genuine unity and peace on earth maybe promoted. For a true education aims at the formation of a human person, with respect to his ultimate goal, and simultaneously with respect to the good of these societies, of which as a man, he is a member, and in whose responsibilities as an adult he will share". The missionaries consequently set up a network of schools through the length and breadth of Manipur and ushered in an 'intellectual revolution'. Education provided them opportunities for personal growth and attainment.

The Christian way of life effected changes in languages and grammar. The first missionaries were painstaking in their efforts to make the tribals master the intricacies of the English language. They taught right pronunciation, enunciation of words and phrases, in short, the niceties of the English language. This enabled the tribals to communicate with the outside world. It provided them the opportunities for career advancement; it enabled them to set new goals for themselves, which were feasible now that they could communicate in a language, which was known as a universal means of communication. Their fluency in the English language received a spurt from their religious education and Christian way of worship, as the Gospel texts and hymns sung in church were largely in English. Mastery of English tongue enlarged their world view, and facilitated learning and understanding in different disciplines.

The Education that the missionaries provided transformed the darkness of illiteracy into the light of literacy. At the time of the advent of the missionaries, the tribals were completely illiterate. The following table depicts the increase in literacy among the tribals, mainly as a result of missionary education.

1981		*2001*	
1. Manipur State	30.05%	Manipur State	47.60%
2. North District	28.81%	Senapati District	36.13%
3. West District	28.08%	Tamenlong District	39.68%
4. South District	36.77%	Churachandpur	49.30%
5. Tengnoupal District	23.93%	Chandel	34.80%

The education enabled the tribals to forge ahead and in fact dominate positions in the civil services, although they benefitted also by the reservation policy of the government.

Some writers have blamed the foreign missionaries outright and have found them responsible for the demise of tribal culture. In so far as cultural songs and dances are concerned, the white missionaries did interfere in some areas. However, the benefits that accrued from the New Faith far more outweigh the loss suffered slightly on the cultural front. Had not the 'Head hunting been turned into Heart hunting through the Love of Christ', the inter-village feuds could, with the introduction of guns and gunpowder by the Britishers, have finished the good customs and culture of the tribes. And had not they imposed education upon the head-hunters through 'forced- labour', the darkness of superstitions could not have been turned into 'Light of Wisdom and Progress'. The old enmities and the spirit of revenge, as the result of Head hunting or otherwise melted away when the unseen 'force' which the local people called the 'Revival' swept the tribal areas of Manipur in early twenties.[65]

The social change brought by Christianity had been far-reaching and overwhelming. It brought a drastic change in food habits. Many new items of fresh vegetables, fruits, pulses and the like were added to the otherwise restricted diet of rice, millet, taro and occasional meat. Milk drinking, once a taboo, became quite popular.[66]

The tribal Christians, just after their conversion, to let people know that they had abandoned the old faith and to remind themselves, that they were changed people, gave up their traditional hair styles. The Tangkhuls hair style was just like 'a cock's comb', whereas for the Kukis, the hair of men was worn long, combed back and tied in a knot on the nape of the neck, which was replaced by the European style.[67] Although the traditional attire of the tribals is resplendent and colourful, under the impact of Christianity and modernization, many converted tribals began to adopt western attire. The transition was facilitated by the fact that the mission schools adopted a western form of dress as school uniforms, shirts, tie, trousers, socks and laced shoes for boys. Skirts, blouses, ties, socks and shoes for girls. As used of western clothes adversely impacted the traditional weaving industry of the tribals, the missionaries set up Grihni Schools teaching tailoring, embroidery etc, and it was the tribal students of these institutions who were given the contract of tailoring the school uniforms. As most, tribal Christians like to dress in formal gowns and suits especially at the time of marriage, training in tailoring and embroidery rendered rich dividends. So also the work of knitting sweaters which were used by school-children.

Though the family was an important unit in tribal society, the real binding force was the clan. It protected the individual but demanded in return obedience and loyalty from him. It was the clan that fostered unity, discipline and group feeling. The reformer-missionary undermined the importance of the clan by making every member suddenly conscious of his individuality. This resulted in the individual placing his own interests above those of the clan or the communities in general.[68]

Marriage in a tribal society was a social institution with a solemn ceremony of religious rites, without which no marriage was considered legal. During the time of pre-Christianity tribal marriage was mostly arranged by the parents and frequent divorce prevailed as a consequence. There was the common practice of paying MOUMAN (bride price) among the tribals. The nature and amount of payment varied from tribe to tribe and it was paid mostly in kind. But this practice of paying bride price has been discontinued among the Christians and has now almost disappeared even among the Non-Christians due to Christian influence. The arranged marriage has gradually given way to love marriage. Consequent to this form of marriage divorce has also disappeared. The practice of levirate was in existence in pre-Christian tribal society. But this practice is now extinct. Polygamy is now wiped out in the tribal society.[69]

The missionaries had always laid stress on the necessity of knowledge. So a number of schools were established in the hills of Manipur. The introduction of education has succeeded in elevating the socio-economic status of the tribal people. The acceptance of a major world religion like Christianity was a major factor of social change in the tribal belt of Manipur. Apart from enthusing the fervor of a new religion, it was responsible for the adoption of Roman script by the tribes, and for an uninhibited pull of tribal culture towards modernization.[70]

The introduction of modern education was so successful that by around 1947 there were around 10,000 educated people and 78 schools in the hills of Manipur. The success of implanting of modern education in the tribes led to the birth of a new educated elite group in the tribal society. This elite group was much more enlightened than the traditional elites; and later on they played a major role in the political life of the tribes.[71]

The spread of Christianity had a profound impact on the socio-economic condition of the tribals. When the tribals converted to Christianity, they discarded all observation of gennas, taboos, merit feasts, practices of sacrifice for sick people, and then the festivals except some like harvest festivals of Kut or Lui-ngai-ni. The converted women were trained in the art of stitching, weaving (modern loom), knitting, neatness and cleanliness, nursing, and so on. The missionaries also introduced carpentry into the hills. The villagers were benefitted by this as they could manufacture their own furniture and construct wooden houses at their own expenses. They also encouraged the people to start fruit farms by supplying seeds of oranges, lemons, apples and others seasonal crops. All these tended to increase in the economic status of the tribes.[72]

The introduction of western way of life through the spread of Christianity led to the development of some undesirable traits in the traditional tribal culture and society. And it is in such negative developments that Christianity faces criticism from certain quarters of tribal society. In the past, the tribal society was bounded by the religious orders of the village. But with the coming of Christianity the converts started defying the traditional religion and subsequently that led to the denouncing of village chiefs and priests. Thus appeared the first chinks in the wall of the village solidarity and gradually the social control of the village based on religion became either nominal or extinct. To remedy this state of affairs the Christian converts of many villages were very often asked to leave the original village if they found it difficult to conform to the village laws, or sometimes it was the Christians themselves who founded a new and all-Christian village to escape the heathen restrictions.[73] The founding of such Christian villages led to the division of the tribal society into Christian and non-Christian villages which was at one time one in all respects.

With the introduction of Christianity, the traditional tribal songs and dances of the tribes lost their importance. Initially these songs and dances were denounced by the missionaries as symbols of paganism. Accordingly, Christian songs in western tunes replaced the traditional songs and dances. Among the younger generation, the guitar has become the symbol of Westernism. In fact the superficial aspect of the western culture have now been here so much confused with Christianity as it is found in this tribal areas of Manipur.[74]

Unlike the other areas of India, the Christian mission was established in Manipur only after the installation of the British colonial administration in the region. Since the creed arrived in Manipur as a concomitant of the colonial rule, it is apparent that missionary activities are viewed as a part of British colonialism. Whatever might be the motive behind the phenomenon but the new creed acted as a powerful agent to change the once static and turbulent tribes of Manipur. Within a comparatively short span of time, there was a drastic transformation of the tribal society in its socio-economic and cultural sphere.

Christianity also brought with it 'Urbanisation'. And in the process of urbanization thousands of individuals are daily leaving their traditional environments in favour of poverty stricken, filthy, shanty towns skirting the larger cities. By moving to the city, the immigrant family gives up much of its old value system and traditional controls of behavior. The overcrowding seriously affects the moral life of the people. The lure of urban settlements has uprooted many of the tribals from their traditional socio-economic set up in the villages. Simultaneously, this migration to urban areas has enabled many tribals to adopt a higher standard of living as a result of better and more varied job opportunities. But many more have been rendered jobless, or forced to do menial jobs in order to eke out a livelihood. Whereas the educated tribal middle class live in well-constructed houses, the have not in tribal society are crowded into low cost housing where very often the basics amenities of running water, sanitation, electricity are not available. This creates a sense of dissatisfaction in many tribals, some of whom then joined movements aimed at assertion of ethnic identity, autonomy, sovereignty etc. and emerge as non-state actors.

It would not be apt if we do not make certain critical observations on the missionary work initiated a century ago.

Early Christian missionaries with their zeal to preach the gospel, labeled the tribal customs as pagan and sinful. The same accusation was heaped upon cultural dances, songs, folklores and the rest, so much so that a section of critics of the Christian missionaries comment that the missionaries must have tried to Westernize, de-tribalise or sanskritise the tribal people.

Whether, consciously or unconsciously, the early missionaries suggested that their way of life was better and superior. Hence, the socio-cultural background of the native population was not taken into consideration. The tribals were forced to feel inferior but they bore the brunt because they thought something good was to follow.

Due to the occurrence of phenomenal changes around the globe-the tribal Christians too have joined the race. 'Individualism' and Consumerism' have become the top priority. The community centred life; the joys of sharing have been relegated to the back bench. Many Christians have become victims to the allurements of the world. They are finding it difficult to maintain the Christians standard of life with all its implications and expectations.

Parental control over the children has diminished over the years. The parent who is often illiterate seems to give undue respect to their growing youth. The Students who go to school and colleges often outsmart their uneducated parents. Therefore the children grow up to be arrogant, unyielding and often became social misfits.

Prior to the Indian independence people obeyed what the village chief or council decided in matters of discipline and justice. Today no one heeds to any authority-everything is interpreted on a convenient hypothesis and strange logistics.

Chinzakham Ngaihte regrets that the absence of morality amongst the youth of our society foreshadows dim future.[75] He continues to say that documents testify the conspicuous presence of high morality among our forefathers in spite of their uncivilized way of life. They did not go through a school, college, or university, but as such, they maintained a good standard of morality. Excessive emulation of the western way of life-without dignity of labour, seriousness and morality is nothing but heading towards a façade of hollow future. We all embraced Christianity as our religion but none of us seem to care for a true Christian life.

Jesus, the protagonist of Christianity seem to have prayed to his heavenly Father that 'all may be one' – meaning that Christians of all races, tribes and nations be known as Christians instead of being known by different denominational names. It has not become a reality.

Even in the State of Manipur, there are over thirty different denominations operating in the name of 'Christ' 'Christianity'. Between those denominations, there is a lot of hostility. In a village if a group of them decide to embrace another denomination, those people are either isolated or segregated from their own kith and kin. They are threatened with dire consequences if they indeed are serious about their new found enthusiasm for another church.

K. Imotemjen Aier shares his opinion on a similar point. He says that the church in North East India is a captive of the 'mission compound' concept. We live in a ghetto; we take pride in the maintenance of some age-long practices in the church imported from the West, which are no longer relevant in our society today.[76] This type of exclusion which was prevalent during the beginning of Christianity, many felt that such individualistic tendencies should not be continued at a time when ecumenicism and coming together of different churches is within the grasp. There has to be a real improvement in this aspect of relationships between different churches operating in Manipur.

In conclusion, and in retrospect, it may be stated that today the things that had happened, and are happening are incredibly true. If any religion can play a vital role in changing the lifestyle of a society, it is Christianity and its mission that have effected this miraculous change among the tribals in Manipur.

REFERENCES

1. Irene, Salam, 'Socio and Cultural life of the Tribals before the advent of Christianity', cit. S. Karotemprel, *The Impact of Christianity on the Tribals of North East India*, Manipur University, 2000.
2. Horam, M., 'William Pettigrew's Contribution to the Reformation of Social Practices of Tribals,' in Rev. William Pettigrew, Pettigrew Centenary Celebration Committee, Manipur. p. 48.
3. Imchen, C. L., *The Nagas and the Legacy of Civilising Mission of the Western World*, D. K. Agencies, Delhi. p. 5.
4. *Ibid.* p. 5.
5. J. Anikuzhikattil, G. Palackapapillel, J. Puthenpurakal, *Understanding Tribal Cultures for Effective Education*, Shillong, 2003. p. 50.
6. *Ibid.*
7. Vaiphei, Rev. S. Prim, *Different Cultural Practices among the Christians in Manipur*, Imphal, 1980. p. 1.
8. Melville, J. Herskarts, *Cultural Anthropology*, Oxford, New Delhi, 1947. p. 305.
9. J. Anikuzhikattil and Co-edited. *Understanding Tribals Cultures, op. cit.* p. 38.
10. Jayaseelan, L., 'Culture an Overview', in *Culture, Mission and Contextualization*, Ed. L. Jayaseelan p. 6.
11. Lyngdoh Sylvanus Sngi, 'The tribal value system and the impact of Christianity on it,' in (Ed.) J. Puthenpurakal, *Impact of Christianity on North East India*, Vendrame Institute Publications, Shillong, 1996.
12. *Ibid.*
13. Aloysius, Nehkhojang T., "The Socio-Cultural life of the Zomis of Manipur," (Ed.) Jayaseelan, L. in *Culture, Mission and Contextualization*, Catholic Manipur Publications, 2000. *op. cit.* p. 54.

14. Lolly, R. R., *The Baptist Church in Manipur*, Manipur Baptist Convention, Imphal, 1985. p. 9.
15. Gangte, T. S., *The Kukis of Manipur*, Gyan Publishing House, New Delhi. Second Edition, 2003. p. 210.
16. Haokip, Peter, 'Folk Culture: A Medium for the Spread of the Gospel', cit. A. Lolsuro: The Nagas, in (Ed.) L. Jayaseelan, *op. cit.* p. 211.
17. J. Anikuzhikattil and Co-edited, *Understanding Tribal Cultures for Effective Education, Op. cit.* p. 54.
18. Haokip Holkhongam, 'Christian Missionaries among the Kukis: A Historical Study', unpublished Ph.D thesis submitted to Manipur University, 2009. p. 19.
19. *Ibid.*
20. J. Anikuzhikattil and Co-edited, *Understanding Tribal Cultures for Effective Education.* p. 94.
21. Laldena, Christian, *Missions and Colonialism*, Shillong, 1988. p. 3.
22. D' Souza Hector, 'A Socio-Anthropological Perspective', (Ed.) L. Jayaseelan, *Culture and Mission and Contextualization.*
23. Mao, Angeline Ariicho, 'Service Oriented Vocations and the tribal Society in North East India', in (Ed.) S. Karotemprel, *The Impact of Christianity on the Tribals of North East India.*
24. Irene Salam, *The Attitude of the Catholic Church towards Society and State in Manipur*, cit. Fr. M. C. George, Rector Don Bosco, Imphal, Manipur University, 2004.
25. *Ibid.*
26. Hector D' Souza *op. cit.* Ed. L. Jayaseelan, *Culture, Mission and Contextualization.* p. 87.
27. Jayaseelan, L., *Impact of the Missionary Movement in Manipur*, Scholar Publishing House, Delhi, 1996. p. 53.
28. *Ibid.* p. 51.
29. Gospel Centenary Souvenir 1910-2010, Published by Celebration Committee, Churachandpur. p. 81.
30. Laldena, *op. cit.* p. 33.

31. *Ibid.*
32. *Ibid.* p. 34.
33. Downs, F. S., *The Mighty Works of God*, Gauhati, 1971. p. 77.
34. *Kristien*, Vol. III No. 1 February 1960. p. 1. (A Monthly Magazine Published by Independent Church of India, Churachandpur).
35. Jayaseelan, L., *op. cit.* p. 54.
36. Gospel Centenary Souvenir 1910-2010, *op. cit.* p. 82.
37. Luikham, T., *A Short History of the Manipur Baptist Christian Golden Jubilee*, 1984. pp. 13-20.
38. Laldena, *op. cit.* p. 37.
39. Luikham, T., *op. cit.* p. 25.
40. *Ibid.*
41. Jayaseelan, L., *op. cit.* p. 54.
42. *Ibid.* p. 26-29.
43. Champang, J., *Christian Life in a Tribal Context in Manipur*, Ukhrul, 1990. p. 33.
44. Jonah, S. M. and Mahangthei, K. (Ed.) *Forty Years in Manipur, Assam* (An Account of the work of W. Pettigrew, the first foreign missionary in Manipur landed in 1894), Imphal, 1986. p. 10.
45. Champang, J. *op. cit.* pp. 38-39.
46. Gospel Centenary Souvenir, *op. cit.* p. 82-83. Watkins Roberts breathed his last in Florida on April 20, 1969 where he and his wife were spending the winter at the Boca Raton Bible Conference. Thus at the age of eighty-three honoured and beloved by all the Zo tribes, Watkin Robert, pioneer missionary and founder of NEIGM, serenely breathed his last.
47. Jayaseelan, L., *op. cit.* p. 84.
48. Gospel Centenary Souvenir, *op. cit.* pp. 90-92.
49. *Ibid.*
50. *Ibid.*

51. Pudaite. Jonathan, *The Legacy of Watkin R. Roberts*, (The pioneer missionary who advocated and empowered indigenous Christian leaders), Partnership Publication Shillong, 2009. p. 58.
52. Jayaseelan, L. (Ed.) Dr. Kamei Gailangam and Dr. Gina Shangkham, *Change and Continuity in the Tribal Society of Manipur*. p. 81.
53. Lolly, R. R., *The Baptist Church in Manipur*. p. 81.
54. *Ibid.*
55. Luikham, T., *A Short History of the Manipur Baptist Christian Golden Jubilee*, Ukhrul, 1948. pp. 4-7.
56. Guite, K. P., 'Development of Education in the Hill areas of Manipur', unpublished thesis submitted to Manipur University, 1991. p. 52.
57. Zarzolien, 'Religious beliefs and practices among the Hmars through the Ages', unpublished thesis submitted to Manipur University, 1987. p. 7.
58. Jayaseelan, L., *op. cit.* p. 123.
59. Sachidanand, *Cultural Changes in Tribal Bihar*, Calcutta, 1964. p. 61.
60. Goswami, Tarun, *Kuki life and lore*, Haflong, 1985. p. 6.
61. Jayaseelan, L. *op. cit.* p. 82.
62. Haokip, Holkhongam, *Christian Missionaries among the Kukis, op. cit.* p. 215.
63. Lolly, R. R., *Op. cit.* p. 71.
64. Irene Salam, *Catholic Education in Manipur*, p. 53 cit. FR. Cervassis, – A Great Herald of Jesus Christ – FR. Aloysius Ravalico.
65. Shimray, R. R., *Origin and Culture of Nagas*, Delhi, 1985. p. 234.
66. Horam, M., *Naga Polity*, Delhi, 1975. p. 134.
67. Lolly, R. R., *Op. cit.* p. 77.
68. Horam, M., *op. cit.* p. 135.
69. Lolly, R. R., *op. cit.* pp. 73-74.
70. Das, S. T., *Tribal Life of North-East India*, Delhi, 1986. p. 292.

71. Champhang, J., *op. cit.* pp. 23-25.
72. Lolly, R. R., *op. cit.* pp. 89-90.
73. Horam, M., *op. cit.* p. 121.
74. Gori, Gulab Khan, *Changing Phase of Tribal Area of Manipur*, Delhi, 1984. p. 99.
75. Chinzakham, L. Ngaihte, 'Is Our Future Hopeful?' In the Young Paite Association Annual Magazine, 1982, Vol. II, p. 26.
76. Imotemjen, Aier K., *A Chance for the Church*, Guwahati, 1982. pp. 21-22.

Two

Culture, Mission and Contextualization

The aims of missionary education have changed with the changes in time. The missionaries have realized the importance of preserving culture. E. B. Taylor defined culture as "that complex vehicle which includes knowledge, belief, art, moral, law, custom and any other capabilities and habits acquired by man as a member of a society.[1]

Culture can be defined as the way of life of a particular society, including its patterns of thought, beliefs, behaviour, customs, traditions, rituals, dress, language, art, music, and literature. These particular systems of beliefs and practices are based on the assumptions people make about themselves, about the world around them and about ultimate realities. Cultures involve the world views, social structures and institutions that give meaning to life. Cultures provide people with the means of expressing their deepest feelings formalised ways understood and accepted by those around them.

Culture is a non-verbal but significant language we must master in order to communicate meaningfully with our target people. No one would think of preaching the Gospel in a language not understood by his audience. A culturally appropriate approach to evangelism is not only a means of making Christianity understandable and attractive to the unconverted, but also of making the local church genuinely indigenous.

Everyone has multiple identities – at times contradictory of nation, race, religion, sect, gender, and language. The wonder of the gospel is that it is offered freely to all assuring them of God's personal love for them in their given context. Christianity does offer liberation from the control and manipulation of oppressive institutions, be they religious, economic, or political. It brings change-but change must be commensurate with one's own culture to prevent alienation.

The Gospel has to be rooted in culture.[2] The Church is universal, yet it is local. The role of culture in mission cannot be underestimated anymore, for culture cannot keep apart from mission, for they co-exist. The church is now interpreting Christ in today's cultural context – liturgy, sacraments, art, architecture, lifestyles.[2]

Most of the history and tradition of the tribal people have been transmitted through the medium of oral tradition. It is only recently that a rich repertoire of this material has been created largely by Christian educated tribals in the form of written literature, history, art, music etc. This fact is best illustrated in the number of written and published works of tribal research students, all educated in Christian schools in the State. Since 'the missionaries are interested in an inculturated way of religious faith, they have facilitated an understanding of the meaning and tenor of folklore. Folklore can be defined as customs, beliefs, stories, traditions etc of a particular group of people, usually passed down through oral tradition.

Inculturation in practice would mean clothing Jesus and His Message in the Idiom and language of the people. The first missionaries came with a zeal, which they only were capable of, to bring spiritual enlightenment to the animistic hill men. Here they ran into difficulties. They would have to work out the bearing of Christianity on the sort of life that was lived in the Naga Hills. The first thing that strikes visitors about the Nagas is their pride and grim loyalty to tradition. The Missionaries had to contend with both, and work out a method, by which the old method and customs could be adopted to suit the new faith they were offering.[3] Culture gives identity to people.

The various communities in the North East face two problems forging a common regional identity in the context of India's polity and capitalist economy; the necessity of reading the inter-regional economic, social and cultural differences.[4]

Religion intertwines itself with culture. God becomes someone who gives meaning to the existence of a particular group of people inhabiting the planet earth.[5] For instance Christian churches are easily recognizable as they represent the culture of the people especially those constructed by the Kuki-Chin and Naga people. Similarly, the traditional dress worn by the tribals to Sunday service is specific to their culture. By introducing new methods of construction, weaving etc. the church has helped in modernising these symbols of native culture. The Christian tribals have not abandoned traditional culture by adopting western dress for daily wear or singing western songs. No doubt, 'colonialisation brought in the process of cultural imperialism.[6] So also the first missionaries decried the heathen culture of the people and initially did much damage to their culture and ways of life. But today, the missionaries are promoting a culture of human solidarity, peace, development based on the principles of native culture. Today, indigenous hymns and dances are incorporated in the Christian liturgy, as cultural tradition is an important vehicle for the transformation of culture. "From the time the Gospel was first preached, the church has known the process of encounter and engagement with cultures.[7] Though inculturation, the church becomes a more intelligible sign of what she is, and a more effective instrument of Mission. The Tribal Christians have greatly helped in this process of inculturation and made the church relevant to the present times by introducing and incorporating appropriate forms of worship in the tribal context. This has fostered co-operation and collective activity in places where peaceful co-operation is the need of the hour. Christian schools open to all have facilitated friendly interchange between students of different backgrounds and cultures.

Tribals have 'a wonderful patrimony of culture, religion and ancient wisdom'.[8] Today the benefits of Christianity and western education have made the tribals aware of their own cultures, with which the missionaries are working creatively by sharing their lives and experiences.

An example of inculturation is the offerings of the produce of fields in church services especially on occasions of weddings, ordinations etc. "All cultures are gifts from God and that in the finite human family cultural diversity reveals the infinity of the creator of that family.[9] "The preservation of Native Identity in the process of Inculturation" in par being a Church in the Modern Society.[10]

While both Christianity and western education have played a role in the modernization of the tribals, the Church too has absorbed elements of modernity by abandoning for instance the western forms of worship and inculcating traditional culture and practices in services and the spread of Gospel in a manner suited to the times. For instance, in the Catholic Church during important occasions and on feasts the offertory procession is preceded by girls dressed in tribal attire, proceeding towards the altar by dancing to traditional tunes and offering the first fruits of their parents labor from their cultivated fields and from the poultry they rear. The Mission is an important factor in culture and civilization.[11]

The Gospel today is interacting with many cultures in the tribal society-all modern culture as for e.g., I.T. culture, consumerist culture, hate culture, culture of violence, of greed etc. Inculturation takes place out of necessity or spontaneously. The Christian faith was enriched with its encounter with the socio-cultural and religious values of the tribals, while simultaneously doing away with inhuman practices like head-hunting, such practices were replaced by modern concepts of living in harmony and fellowship. Christianity by giving special focus to the poor and marginalised brought them into the mainstream where they too could benefit from modernization, whether in the field of education, animal husbandry, poultry farming etc. The Church did not insist on one lifestyle, or custom or special place of worship. "Christians are not distinguished from the rest of mankind by their country, speech or customs.[12]

Oneness of creation and land are key elements of tribal world view and they affect every sphere of human life: social, economic, cultural and religious. Many elements are similar to the Biblical perspective and Inculturation the Gospel.[13]

Since tribals are from different communities, the church supports and encourages pluralism in accordance with the definition of "Inculturation seeks to naturalize the church in every country, region and social sector", in Manipur the Christianity which contributed to modernizing the tribals, did so not initially, but in course of time by respecting their native genius and their character. Inculturation and contextualization has brought about transformation in the tribal human cultures. It is said that when the pioneer Baptist Missionaries in Mizoram

J. H. Lorrain and F. W. Savidge preached Jesus Christ as 'Saviour from Sin' they made no impression on the people. However when they proclaimed Jesus as 'the Vanquisher of the Devil' it was good news indeed and exactly met their need.'[14]

In endeavouring to develop a proper tribal Christology, the missionaries are making an exhaustive study of tribal culture and also presenting it in a way conducive to the lives. The Bible is particularly responsive to a tribal interpretation (steeped in tribal culture). So the teaching of Jesus can be seen as a return to the tribal ethos.[15] Prayer and Hymns are sung in the traditional way, strengthening tribal folk-culture. The Christian missionaries through inculturation are promoting and improving the folk culture of the tribal people i.e. their inborn talent, skill and love for music. Since inculturation requires a close association and association with indigenous spiritual tradition, the missionaries have and are familiarising themselves with indigenous scriptures that contain the spiritual experiences of the people. Most of the Christian clergy today are indigenous tribals, although quite a many have widened their world view by their studies and research in places and countries outside of Manipur. They are also creating atmosphere of freedom and trust to facilitate the emergence of the creative forces of the people, and establishing inter-religious dialogue, to bring unity among tribes warring with one another. By creating awareness about the blatant disrespect for human life, they are trying to bring about peace, justice and reconciliation.

There are different components in the folksongs of all tribes. First music varies depending on the nature of the song. Second, they contain the treasure of literature of the people, third- depiction of people's philosophy of life and fourth- depiction of personal characters in the historical traditional songs. After embracing Christianity, many of the original lyrics containing romantic and derogative expressions in many traditions have been modified to the tune of the gospel message. The traditional dances express the depth and extent of a people's meaningful system. They continue to reveal new insights even in the present time. There is a common season for everything. The principle of this synchronic solidarity remains unchanged. The pulling of the village gate or monolith, the call for social work the women society of a church community – all these are organized synchronically in a spirit of solidarity. The sense of 'otherness' has no place in a tribal system of order. It is interesting to analyse the back and forth rhythmic movements of Naga and Kuki-Chin dances. The pace of social and economic development also keeps the same pattern of progress and digresses.[16]

A tribal way of reading the parable of the treasure and of the pearl in Matthews Gospel (13: 44-46) can be described "A man finds a treasure hidden in the fields goes off in his joy, sells everything he owns and buys the field". The hidden treasure is the education in English medium schools. The tribal man finds it and sells everything he owns and gives it to the schools as tuition fees and the remainder to his child as pocket money.[17] Tradition has combined with modernity apparent in the integration of the social perspective of the tribals with the Gospel perspective.

Christology in fact becomes highly relevant to contextualisation, since those who want to make the context determinative for the meaning of what Christ said have a 'Christology from below', that is they begin with the human Jesus and focus on his life and words. They bring their own human context to his context, to see how he can inspire and encourage them. Those who have a 'Christology from above' tend to view his words in terms of absolutes, which need no interpretation and are relevant to every context. The Incarnation broke through any division between the eternal and the human.

It does not destroy the difference between them, but it does allow us to hold the two together. Similarly text and context need to be held together to be faithful to God's revelation in Christ. To relativise the text is to lose its transcendent dimension. To absolutise the text is to make it irrelevant. Just as Christ was, Christians are 'in the world, but not of the world' and therefore are a 'pilgrim people' whose identity arises out of, and sets its sight upon, transcendent realities. "Not only does God in Christ take people as they are, He takes them in order to transform them into what He wants them to be. Along with the indigenizing principle, which makes his faith a place to feel at home, the Christian inherits the pilgrim principle, which whispers to him that he has no abiding city and warns him that to be faithful to Christ will put him out of step with his society; for that society never existed, in East or West, ancient time or modern, which could absorb the word of Christ painlessly into its system".

Our contextualization must follow Christ as an 'incarnation' both of the gospel and of our own selves. As we do that we will find both being transformed and at the same time the context itself renewed in line with God's truth.

WHAT IS CONTEXTUALIZATION?

Contextualization is the way we respond sensitively to the variety of cultures, following the Biblical precedents. OM's "Book of Standard Definitions" states that Contextualization is: "The effort to understand and take seriously the specific context of each human group and person on its own terms and in all its dimensions – cultural, religious, social, political, economic – and to discern what the gospel says to people in that context." Further it states that it is "the attempt to communicate the message of the person, works, Word, and will of God in a way that is faithful to God's revelation, especially as it is put forth in the teachings of Holy Scripture, and that is meaningful to respondents in their respective cultural and existential contexts".[18]

These statements point to the various elements inherent in the concept of contextualization: the variety of human cultures, God's unchanging message, and our duty to communicate that message in a way that can be understood by the recipients.

Contextualization means that we realise that just as sin is pervasive in all cultures (including our own), so the image of God, though distorted, is present in men of all cultures. God condemns sin in all cultures in its many varying forms, and puts his witness into each culture so all may find Him. God has not left himself without a witness in any culture – there are hidden Gospel keys and redemptive analogies in all cultures waiting to be discovered and used in opening hearts and breaking down barriers.

There has been a lot of controversy in the missionary world over contextualization, much discussion over the meaning of the term, its implications, ways of implementation, and inherent dangers.

The need to confess that one's own home church systems and theologies that feel comfortable with contain much that is not primal Biblical truth, but contextualized interpretations and adaptations of that truth to Hellenistic, Roman, and Western European cultures developed over almost two millennia. True contextualization can only begin when there is an honest examination of our own Christian culture and background, separating the wheat of Biblical truth from the chaff of traditions and cultural mores. The same freedoms can be accepted for the church in our culture, which ought to allow believers in other cultures too.

Contextualization shows respect for others different from us. They are just as worthy or unworthy in God's eyes. We are no better than just as lost as they are, except for God's grace in Christ. We must move away from paternalism, hegemony, ethnocentrism, and racism by practicing a love that breaks down barriers, is incarnation, willing to suffer, and accepts the culture of the ones we are called to serve.

Acceptation of what is true and good in all cultures and reject what is false and evil in each. The Bible must be the ultimate criterion for our faith and practice, our beliefs, norms, and rituals.

MEANINGFUL COMMUNICATION OF GOSPEL

No one would think of preaching the Gospel in French to the Chinese, or in Hindi to the Nigerians. Culture is a language that has to be learned like any other in order to communicate clearly and convey the true meaning of the Gospel in terms understood by the recipients. Knowing and sensitively using culture is as vital as translating the Bible into people's languages. The Gospel must be expounded in culture-specific ways, using what is known and familiar to introduce what is new and unknown. Just as we invest a lot of effort in learning the language of our target group, so we must also invest much effort in learning their culture.

We must be aware that there might be a multiplicity of cultures in a given state, and that cultures may change gradually over time. Secularized and westernised urban elites may be quite happy with western Christian forms. Yet even they often have a deep down emotional subconscious attachment to their own religion/cultural norms.

Contextualization means a search for the ways people communicate with each other, and the ways meanings, feelings, experiences, and relationships are expressed. These insights are then used both in the communication of the gospel, and in the new church's structures, customs, and rituals that symbolise its deepest understanding of the meaning of God's truth. The indigenous cultural colouring helps individuals escape alienation, and the church survives long-term among its own people.

People love their own cultures and will not accept what does not make sense to them, so if the missionaries reach out to them within the context of their own culture, realising that all cultures can adequately serve as vehicles for communicating the Gospel. The Good News is not addressed to a theoretical humanity, but to real human beings in specific situations at specific times. The gospel is presented in a meaningful way to each culture, building on indigenous terms, idioms, and cultural forms modified to fit its worldview. Drawing on the Bible, Jesus is presented in his different aspects (Messiah, Lord, Saviour, Redeemer, High Priest, Prophet, King, Logos, Word Of God, Son, Mediator, Peace-Maker, etc.) as fulfilling all divine roles and human needs expressed in the specific culture of Manipur's tribals.

Sensitively applied, contextualization shows the local followers of Christ that they do not need to reject much of their culture in order to be saved and lead the life of true disciples of Jesus. Both theology and practice are contextualized without losing their Biblical essence – only the oppressive and anti-Biblical components of indigenous culture are rejected.

The goal is not a uniform one world religion, but a multitude of disciples from every tongue, tribe, and nation, praising and glorifying God within their own cultures. With all their variety, they truly represent God's Kingdom on Earth and the Body of Christ to those around them as they live by the power of the Holy Spirit in obedience to Scripture. Cultural forms are transformed to become Spirit filled vehicles that channel new life into the local congregations and out into the community.

HOW TO CONTEXTUALIZE?

According to Hiebert, neither wholesale rejection (the mistake of colonial missionaries), nor uncritical acceptance (the modern liberal approach) are appropriate. The Biblical approach is that of critical contextualisation. This means an acceptance of the necessity of contextualisation, followed by a sympathetic study of cultural rites and traditions. These are then evaluated critically in the light of Biblical teaching by the people involved, who will then make the decision of what to keep, what to reject, what to modify, and what to accept from other cultures. They might even decide to create some totally new forms appropriate to their understanding.

The involvement of the converts is absolutely necessary, as only they know the real and deep meaning and symbolism of their cultural traditions. It is also a practical affirmation of the Biblical principles of the Priesthood of every believer, and of the Spirit dwelling in every believer and guiding him to the truth. The missionaries have no monopoly on either priesthood or the Holy Spirit. This paradigm allows the new church and its members to grow and mature as they grapple with both the scriptures and their culture and engage in a prayerful encounter with the underlying meanings of both. They can then boldly face their own people with a clear presentation of the good news in a culturally meaningful way.

CONVERTS AND CHURCHES

Converts need all the help, encouragement, and counsel that the missionaries provide, especially the indigenous clergy. Choice gives them a sense of self-identity and dignity. Converts need role models to follow – experience shows they always follow the model of those who helped them to the new faith. That is why it was so important for missionaries to adapt to the local culture and contextualise the gospel, so as to prevent alienation of converts and the local church from their own people.

Manipur is a State plagued by unrest, strife, alienation, violence, a consequence of modernization as also other related factors. For instance, modernity made tribals conscious of their identity and this in course of time lead to first ethnic consciousness and then national consciousness and set in motion movements to attain individual autonomy or sovereignty, through both peaceful and violent means. This causes people either to look outside their own traditions for identity, or else to turn ever more inward towards their own roots and authentic traditions. Some turn to a superficial Westernization that can leave them rootless. Others become radical "fundamentalists" seeking to impose their utopian view of an ancient "golden age" on their societies. All tribal Christians need to understand these currents and utilise them for sharing the gospel message. They may need to tailor their message differently to different tribal communities in the state. Often minorities are more likely to adopt a religion different to that of the majority in order to preserve their distinctive identity from the threat of assimilation and extinction.

The church needs to take root more firmly in its local society and become indigenous, to counter the trend of converts becoming alienated from their own people and emigrating to the West where they assume they will be more advantaged because of the benefits of modernity. Expatriates need to go beyond a superficial knowledge of language to studiously observe the host culture and understand its essence. This needs time and training, but will enable them to be more sensitive to their religious and cultural traditions and values.

CRITIQUE OF CONTEXTUALIZATION

The greatest danger is that of syncretism, of departing from Biblical truth and incorporating evil and oppressive elements into the local Church practice and theology. Whilst this danger is real, it is also true that it has been used as a red flag by western evangelicals convinced of the superiority of their own culture to that of the people they were working with. Western Churches face these very same dangers within their own cultures and all have to constantly battle against them.

Whilst contextualizatiom might help attract some people, the core religious power holders of a given culture might never accept Christianity as a tolerated competitor and manipulate the state to annihilate the Church. This however might happen even faster when Christianity remains a visible foreign body in that culture.

Host cultures might be changing and looking for forms that symbolize freedom from traditional restraints as they try to adapt to modernity. It is necessary to be sensitive to such shifts and offer a variety of models to the various tribal communities. Believers insulated in a very conservative culture with very limited contact with other Christians might not realise their relationship to the universal church. However patience is required to realise the goal and for the native Church to achieve maturity.

Contextualization can become a barrier blocking converts from the complete experience of Christ. This might be due to a lack of complete acceptance of Jesus as the final and authoritative mediator of God's will, of seeing Jesus as just one of a number of supernatural mediators, or to a lack of complete acceptance of Christ's perfect atoning work by a stress on the necessity of "right" religious rites to attain acceptance by God. The lack of complete acceptance of salvation through grace and by faith alone, using ritual and forms as an added insurance, can be a real danger. It is a danger faced also by churches in the west, when regardless of written creeds they develop behavioural norms that serve as criteria for true belonging.[19]

Despite earnest endeavours to create a truly local church some obstacles remain as some rituals are foreign to the tribals. For instance:

Baptism – Baptism by water can be substituted by an equivalent initiation as for instance with the Holy water sprinkled in church on the faithful is like the water sprinkled over a sacrifice by the tribal priest in indigenous culture.

Homogeneity – A homogeneous Christian church is more stable and deep rooted but simultaneously it causes fissures in tribal society as each tribe names the church after themselves eg. Tangkhul Baptist Church, Kuki Baptist Church, Tangkhul Catholic Association etc. Many see it as a betrayal of the universality of the church, yet often attend their own native tribal Christian Church.

Forms of Worship – can be made more culture specific – a beginning has already been made especially with the induction of large numbers of native missionaries.

Many contexts, references, passages which are contextualized are not part of the original Scriptures, as the definitions applied to the Trinity and the person of Christ.

Effort must be made to clothe these terms in native form to make it more relevant to the lives of the tribals.

The missionaries especially the western missionaries failed to differentiate between gospel and culture and equated the gospel with their own culture. This led to condemnation of indigenous customs and imposition of Western culture on converts, and was used to justify Western imperialism, ethnocentrism, pride, and wrong comparisons. Fortunately, the indigenous clergy are actively engaged in rooting the Church in the native culture.

The Supernatural – However, because of the centuries old belief of the tribals in benevolent and malevolent spirits, these beliefs need to be handled sensitively when they are replaced by the Christian concept of Angels and demons. Liberation achieved by accepting Christ as personal Saviour does not give license to the tribal Christians to force their modern ideas and ways of life on those who prefer to retain their indigenous religion and old ways of life. These are to be inculcated and made compatible with modernity but not condemned.

CONCLUSION

To begin with, the early days of Christianity in Manipur, the local people's experience with the missionaries was simply a matter of distinction "who we were" and "who they were". We were different groups of ethnic people engrossed in our own cultural mores. The missionaries were white people coming from a distant land to baptize us to their fold. What did we have and what did they have? We had our land, our culture, and an entirely different world view. The missionaries instead had the Holy Bible, medicines and a package of educational programmes. They had a powerful mechanism to wake us from the deep slumber in a narrow, illiterate world. Upon their arrival we gazed at them with expectant eyes. Every society is transformed at different stages of its history. Initially Christianity and education transformed tribal society, but for the momentum to be sustained, the focus has in recent decades shifted to Inculturation, Mission and Contextualization.

REFERENCES

1. Melville, J. Herskovits, *Cultural Anthropology*, Oxford, New Delhi, 1974. p. 305.
2. Foreword of Most Rev. Joseph Mittathany DD, Archbishop of Imphal, 2000 in Jayaseelan, L. (Ed.), *Culture, Mission and Contextualization*, p. vii.
3. Irene Salam, *Catholic Education in Manipur*, cit. p. 2, M. Horam, *Social and Cultural Life of the Nagas*. p. 13.
4. Kamei, Gangmumei, *On History and Historiography of Manipur*, Akansha Publishing House, 2006. p. 79.
5. Jeyaseelan, L. (Ed.), 'Culture an Overview', in *Culture, Mission Contextualization*. p. 6.
6. Jeyaseelan, *Ibid.* p. 11.
7. Archbishop Joseph Mittathany. D. D., *Churches Pastoral Approach to Culture*, in L. Jayaseelan. (Ed.), *Culture, Mission and Contextualization*. p. 62.
8. D' Souza. Hector, Dr., "A Socio-Anthropological Perspective," p. 77. *Ibid.* L. Jeyasaleen, *Culture and Mission and Contextualization*.
9. Jayaseelan, L., *The Necessity of Inculturation in Gospel Proclamation*, *op. cit.* p. 90, cit. T. Zuern.
10. Gollius, A. A. (Ed), *Rome*, Pontifical Gregorian University, 1983. pp. 6-11.

11. Lal Dena – *Christian Mission and Colonialism*, p. 6. cit. Von Walter Holsten 'Kolonalismusals Theologisches Problem' in Stat Crux dumcrolvitur...., p. 163.
12. The Epistle to Diognets quoted in G. M. Soares, *Prabhu*, 1976, p. 281.
13. Manjaly, Thomas Dr., *Inculturating the Gospel: Some Biblical Models*, in L. Jayaseelan (Ed.), *Culture, Mission and Contextualization*. 2000, p. 112.
14. Thanzaua CF and R. L. Hnuni, 'Ethnicity, Identity and Humanities: on India Tribal Perspective,' in M. G. Brett (Ed.), *Ethnicity and the Bible*, New York, 1996. p. 348.
15. Soaras, G. M., *Prabhu, Tribal Values in India*, Jeevadhaea, 24:140, 1994, p. 84,
16. Linus, Neli, In Search of Christ Experience through Culture, in L. Jayaseelan (Ed.), *Culture, Mission and Contextualization*. pp. 163-165.
17. Linus, Neli, *Ibid.* L. Jayaseelan (Ed.) *op. cit.* p. 17.
18. Bradshaw, Bruce, "Integrity and Respect Are Keys to Muslim Witness", *EMQ*, October, 1988.
19. Teeter, David, "Dynamic Equivalence Conversion for Tentative Muslim Believers," *Missiology*, Vol. XVIII, No. 3, July, 1990.

Three

The Impact of Modern Education

The one single foremost agent of social change is education. This is particularly true of North East India where the levels of Primary School, High School, Higher Secondary College and University education were among the lowest in India, both in quality and quantity. Before the advent of colonial rule and the Christian Missionaries the tribal people of North East India did not have the tradition of formal education both in the family and society. The influence of education on tribal people cannot be over estimated. It is education that more than anything else shaped the new tribal society. Education moulded the entire human society in a new frame.[1] Education is a creative force, which supplies new ideas, transforming the mindsets of the society, and which has far reaching effects on society. It can also alter, reform, reconstruct, and revitalize the social fabric that prevails. The main agent for the transformation of human thinking is education. It also brings the realization that a society to be strong has to be united.[2]

Ever since the establishment of British Political Agency in Manipur in 1835, the Agents worked to introduce Primary education among the Manipuris. Such an initiation from the

Political Agents was made possible by the legislation in 1813 in British Parliament for the spread of education in India. The Agitation for such legislation was led by one Charles Grant the Father of Modern Education in India.[3] But as the Meiteis in the Manipur valley had been newly converted to Hinduism (albeit in the 17th century) they were strongly suspicious of western education and mistakenly believed that they might be converted to Christianity, or that their daughters would be sent outside the State for education or that they may be forced to eat meat and prohibitory dietary items. The pioneering work was an uphill task for the Political Agents, and their initial efforts were not crowned with success. Pioneers like Major General W. E. Nuthall, Sir James Johnstone, Rev. W. Pettigrew and His Highness Maharaj Chandrakriti Singh worked for the growth of Primary education in Manipur. But in spite of their efforts the progress of Primary education was very slow for a long time even after annexation of Manipur (1891) because of the native attitude of the local people towards western education.[4]

The Manipuris had their own indigenous system of education, but their suspicious attitude towards western education took a long time to change, and it was only after Manipur's merger with India (1949) that rapid strides were made in education. In the beginning, they had an indifferent attitude to western education. They considered the Sahibs (Britishers) as 'untouchable' or 'impure'. So the western education disseminated by them was also treated as impure.[5]

Education and Missionary work in the context of North East India seem to go hand in hand. A hundred years ago, the people in the region were illiterate and the early missionaries realized that if they were to be successful in spreading the Gospel message, they would have to start teachings the 3 'R's.

The seed of English education was first shown by Capt. Gordon when he organised a primary education centre in

Manipur in the beginning of the 19th century. Due to the untimely death of Capt. Gordon, the seed could not germinate. In 1872, Major General W. F. Nuthall, the then Political Agent opened a school at Imphal with English language as the medium of instruction. For this, the Government of Bengal presented books, maps and other requisites of the value of ₹ 500. But the school did not function properly due to want of local co-operation or encouragement. The people of the land did not appreciate the establishment of English schools, and had no love and fancy for English education, and as such the parents did not send their children to that school.[5]

But in the closing part of the 19th century circumstances changed, the number of Britishers in the State increased, and the deep feeling of untouchability towards foreigners slowly subsided. The first missionary was Pettigrew who came in the closing years of the 19th century. Maharaj Chandrakriti gave his consent to Sir James Johnstone for establishing an English School. The King allotted a plot of land where the school building was constructed. Thus Sir James Johnstone established an English School in 1885 at Imphal which is now known as Johnstone Higher Secondary School. During 1893-94, two L. P. Schools and Pettigrew L. P. School were established.

Later, English education and William Pettigrew became almost synonymous with regard to the growth of education in Manipur. As soon as he reached Imphal, he made the necessary preparation for advancing education and literacy among the people. The people in the plains found it extremely difficult to adapt themselves to the new ideas and ways of life.

Being anxious, to spread education as widely as possible especially as his primary mission was to convert the people to Christianity, Pettigrew gave private tuition to the children of government servants. He also opened an ideal school, by writing books in Manipuri, and taught them in his school. A Manipuri dictionary and some other textbooks are his outstanding and unforgettable works. Because of his educational efforts, the State authorities appointed him as Honorary Inspector of Schools for 7 (seven) years from 1897-1903.[6]

Despite the sincere efforts of the British Political Agents to disseminate western education in Imphal, many Meiteis in the valley were against sending their children to English medium schools. The few parents who dared to do so exhibited courage but simultaneously ensured that anything associated with English education was kept out of the main House. The children had to change their uniform, keep their books and other School items in a shed that adjoins almost all Meitei houses. They thought that uncleanliness and evil spirits might be brought in to the house by such association and education. Some parents even performed certain rituals to purify the children attending a Mission school.

When education first spread to the hills, the attitude of the elders towards those who went to school was that they were lazy. The slur of laziness was cast on the grounds that in comparison to the arduous back-breaking labor in the fields, the attendance in School was a 'breeze' and did not entail any physical labour at all. No attention was paid to developing mental abilities and honing one's intellect. All were expected to go to the field and do hard work and not sit under shady roofs and wile away the time.[7] T. Luikham admits, "Our fathers living in caves and jungles were blind to the advantage of education and averse to its introduction. But the untiring efforts of Mr. Pettigrew brought about a lasting effect on the younger generation".[8]

The animosity of the people towards the colonial administrators and Christian Missionaries was born out of the fear, that education would result in the young people severing ties with their villages to the extent that they may not even return home after exposure to the outside world. But once the people realized the sincerity of the missionaries in their zeal to discipline and educate the native children, opposition waned. Gradually there came about a realization that education effects revolutionary change and leads children on the parts of progress and development.[9]

Today, there is a sea change in the tribal people's attitude towards mission education. Everyone admits of its worth in manifold ways. The western education rapidly transformed the society. Since then every effort was directed towards acquiring a sound education. The preference of the tribals for education in Christian missionaries institutions is due to several factors: Firstly, the major part of the tribal population converted to Christianity in the 19th century, Secondly, It was the Christian especially Catholic Missionaries who set up a network of Schools all over the hill areas and brought literacy to the people. Thirdly, the State government paid little or no attention to providing the necessary infrastructure for education in the hill areas. In contrast, Christian missionaries have set up Colleges in recent times in the hill districts, with the intention of expanding the network of higher educational institutions. The missionaries also provided education to all in the hills – the haves and the have not. As a result, many tribals who availed of this education attained high positions in society and State. A lot of officers for instance, in the IAS Manipur cadre would illustrate this fact. There are around fifty tribals IAS officers from Manipur. Some tribals of different ethnic origin were given the opportunity to pursue higher studies especially theology in the United States, United Kingdom, Rome etc.[10] As a result of exposure to the outside world through education the tribals gave up their insular attitude, and familiarized themselves with new ideas, thoughts, value, philosophy, way of life etc. The missionaries also provided them with new job opportunities such as teachers, pastors, deacons, catechists, social workers etc. By enabling the individual to acquire, a sustainable means of livelihood, the missionaries fostered a spirit of independence among the tribals and enabled them to stand on their own feet. Their increased earnings raised their standard of living.

At present, at least 90 per cent of the hill tribal population is Christian. All groups of Nagas and Kuki-Chins of Manipur have adopted Christianity. The remarkable achievement has been the result of the spread of education.[11] The tribals are proud to be Christians and their religious devotion and exuberance is manifest in the numerous religious conferences and allied activities that are held all over the state throughout the year.

Education was an essential element for successful evangelism in the underdeveloped areas, particularly in the hill areas of Manipur, where the people were quite ignorant of education. For the missionaries and to be more specific, the Protestant missionaries, often exalted the bible as the ultimate source of authority and made it a pre- condition that if an individual had to worship God right, he must be able to read. This is how education and evangelism were interlinked and the former constituted the basis for the '*prepaertio evangelic*'. Therefore, the involvement of missionaries in educational programmes is to be viewed as a supplement to the primary task of spreading the Gospel message. The missionaries considered the three R's as the most effective means for winning adherents to the faith and also for enabling them to learn the basic tenets of the Christian faith. According to them, educational institutions serve a double purpose; first, it was a means of teaching the Christian faith, and secondly, a means for recruitment or training for future service to the mission as well as to the State.[12]

Rev. W. Pettigrew the first Christian missionary arrived in Imphal in 1894-95, and being, refused permission to do missionary work in the valley, he kindly undertook the work of supervising education in Manipur State. He began by holding private tutorial classes. In those days, there was no good school in Imphal. The present Johnstone Higher Secondary School was the only U. P. school but it catered to a small minority and was not available for all the people. The medium of instruction was also in Bengali. Pettigrew in consultation with the state authorities opened an ideal school at Singjamei (Chingamakha). He having acquired proficiency in the Manipuri tongue wrote a Manipuri Primer, a Manipuri grammar, some textbooks and English-Bengali-Manipuri Dictionary and some other books in order to facilitate the spread of education. He laid a solid foundation for modern education in Manipur. Within a year, his school surpassed previously established institutes. The state authorities and the public were satisfied and pleased with his sincere, whole-hearted, and tireless work for the upliftment of the people of Manipur.[13] Impressed by his moral influence and expertise, Maxwell, the then Political Agent had appointed him as honorary Inspector of Schools by entrusting him with the power to draw up the whole educational budget for the entire state.[14]

But soon Pettigrew had to discontinue his work in Imphal as the people and as also the Maharajah of Manipur were suspicious of his intentions and wanted him to be removed from the Imphal valley. The British authorities were sensitive to these sentiments of the orthodox Hindu-Manipuris, who were averse to missionary activities in the valley. Pettigrew was asked to shift his place of work and he moved to Ukhrul in January 1896, which was one of the biggest villages of the Tangkhul tribes.[15] But he remained in touch with the educational establishments in the state and continued to supervise the education work. As a follow up to his supervision and advice, an Inspecting Pandit, a Manipuri from Cachar (Assam), was appointed to visit and constantly inspect all the primary schools in the valley. As a result, Mr. Pettigrew, on his last tour of inspection, reported a great improvement in the educational standards of all the schools.[16]

The first action of Pettigrew in Ukhrul was to start a school, and accordingly in February 1897 a Middle English school was opened at that village. But he faced difficulties in getting students. The children as well as the parents were reluctant to avail of modern education. In fact, nearly six weeks were spent by the missionary in persuading the villagers to send at least twenty of their boys to School. Ultimately, it was through the intervention of the Political Agent and under threat of punishment, that the first batch of students was sent. The villagers fearing the Government's reprisal, selected the first batch of boys from every clan of the village.[17]

On February 19, 1897, the school opened with 21 boys including the village Chief Raihao, who also acted as Pettigrew's teacher at night, teaching him the Ukhrul dialect. The names of the students were: 1. H. A. Raihao, 2. Hamring 3. Mapha 4. Kuipang 5. Heitheng 6. Sakho 7. Ramkaiphang 8. Yarnao 9. Pheikho 10. Hollei 11. Phungsan 12. Yuishi 13. Maninglum 14. Sangmayang 15. Kaphungkui 16. Thisan 17. Mangaleng 18. Shangam 19. Sakhayang 20. Fasing 21. Leishisan.[18]

Hesitant and suspicious at first, the people's attitude changed slowly but surely, when they witnessed the transformation effected in school children-in matters of knowledge, discipline, value system etc. The parents gradually started sending their children to the school. And by the time when the Pettigrew's took their first furlough (1903) a total of 57 boys had been enrolled in the school. From 1895 to 1903, Mr. Pettigrew in the capacity of Honorary Inspector of schools supervised the establishment of State schools in various parts of the capital and in different sections of the valley. He also secured and appointed teachers, arranged the curriculum, prepared with the help of Manipuri teachers who had been educated in Assam the many textbooks needed, and visited the valley twice a year on inspection tours. So when he relinquished the post in 1903, 28 schools had been established, including two Upper Primary schools in Naga inhabited areas, one at Mao and another at Ukhrul. And 23 textbooks were translated from Bengali into Manipuri. The state bore expenses of all this work.[19] His literary works were a great boon and acted as an answer to literary needs of modern education in Manipur.

In 1903, another school was established at Hundung (Ukhrul sub division). Between, 1896-1905, progress was spectacular. Within this short period, 8 Lower Primary schools were opened in the Tangkhul areas and he could enroll 38 boys. At that time, Pettigrew was acting both as a missionary and as an officiating State Officer in all matters effecting the day-to-day administration of the hills. So in the latter capacity, he ensured that the 10 schools received aid from the State Govt. Ukhrul became a centre of education and students came from different hill areas of Manipur to study there. Till very recently the rate of literacy in the Tangkhul hills was higher than in other tribal areas. Inevitably, many of the students embraced christianity.[20]

Among the students R. Riuchumhao Tangkhul, who hailed from Somdal village, was the first to complete his high school education from among the hill tribes. He was appointed as the Headmaster of Ukhrul Mission M. E. School 1920. Then he was appointed Area Superintendent of Western Tangkhul in 1921. In the same year, a Mission Centre Lower Primary School was opened at Somdal. And later this school was upgraded to an M. E. school. Students came from different villages and from other tribes' too.[21]

Apart from the regular classes in the mission school as an effective programme of evangelism, classes were also held on Sundays, known as Sunday school classes. These were based on regular Bible lessons, which were introduced in various schools and in the local church at Ukhrul. Both Christians and non-Christians were invited to the Sunday school classes and taught the Bible stories. As per the statistics in Mr. Pettigrew's Report of 1907, there was one organized Local Church (possibly the Ukhrul local church) with 35 members. Apparently, there were nine other places also where regular Sunday school classes were organized. Thus, many non- Christians were taught Bible stories and scriptures lessons.[22] This familiarity with the Bible teachings led them in course of time to convert to Christianity.

Efforts were also made by the missionaries to educate the tribal girls. But when the local people had looked with suspicion upon any attempt to educate their sons how much more strongly did they oppose the education of girls; Girls were meant to work at home and assist in the rice fields. So education would serve no purpose for girls. It took Mr. Pettigrew fourteen years to make an appreciable impression, even after the parents had converted. As parents were reluctant to allow girls to free themselves from domestic chores in the daytime, Pettigrew's wife Alice hit on the idea of starting a night school for girls. This was feasible once a village had allowed the opening of a school for boys; the teacher's then urged the parents to permit their daughters after the day's work was done to attend the night schools. Later Mr. Pettigrew persuaded girls from villages to come to Ukhrul to study. Here they were taught not only to read and write, but living in a small dormitory, they were taught the art of housekeeping, importance of sanitation, personal hygiene and also imparted vocational skills like sewing and knitting, gardening, cultivating, weeding and harvesting in a more scientific, methodical manner. In short, they were made to do all the work they would have to do when they returned home.[23]

The formation of women's society and education for women was another major contribution of the missionary to the growth of education in Manipur. In May 1930, Mr. Pettigrew wrote a comprehensive letter for circulation among missionary friends. In it, he wrote that there were "two M. E. schools with 70 girls and 156 boys on the rolls, 30 primary schools with 150 girls and 408 boys, and one K. G. school with 14 girls and 6 boys". In a sense, this letter explained the achievement of the missionary in the field of education in the hills of of Manipur. These Primary schools were spread throughout the state, but mostly in Christian villages only. Excepting the Kangpokpi and the Ukhrul M. E. schools, the other schools were not supported by the Mission. The villagers themselves supported and paid all expenses for the running of the schools in their villages out of local church funds. Eventually, each village had its own school which shows the progress of education among the tribals.[24] This was due to the humanitarian service rendered by the missionaries.

By 1938, 7 male teachers and 1 female teacher were working in the Kangpokpi M. E. School run by the American Baptist Mission. On the 30th June of the same year there were 88 boys and 40 girls on the rolls. In the Ukhrul M. E. School, there were 3 masters, with 67 boys and 6 girls on the rolls on the 30th June, 1938. In addition to Ukhrul, it had 37 Primary schools in the villages employing 41 teachers. There were 527 boys and 120 girls on the rolls at the close of the year. 12 boys and 4 girls received scholarships in the High school and 3 girls studying in the Nurses training school. The school also enjoyed grant-in-aid of ₹ 1500/- from the State Government of Manipur. The North East India General Mission (N.E.I.G.M) worked in Southern Manipur and maintained 1 English Bible school at Churachandpur. In addition to this school, the mission also maintained 21 permanent village schools and some temporary village schools.[25]

The turn of events during the second quarter of the 20th century, the introduction of western education in Manipur had become quite different from the preceding years; the Kukis (Chin-Kuki-Mizo) inhabited area, the present Churachandpur District, too no longer remained untouched by the light of the Gospel and modern education. For the hill people, Education and Christianity were synonymous and the one who got either of these was enlightened, whereas those who were not so inclined continued to live as before. While attempting to trace the events or circumstances that led to bringing about modern education to the Kuki-chin-Zomi areas the name of Rev. Watkin Roberts, a young Welsh missionary could not but come in the forefront. It was in 1910, the Rev. Watkin Roberts sent a printed literature, the text of Gospel according to St. John from the Bible to various parts of the Lushai Hills. A copy of it happened to reach the chief of Senvon village, which is situated at the corner of the border between the Lushai Hills and the state of Manipur. That spark of the Gospel became the enlightening flame for all the Kuki-Chin of the District. As elsewhere, when the missionaries were to propagate the Gospel they used the means of education as their first step to achieve their goal, At Senvon too, a mission school came up in 1911 with the following persons as the staff, namely Savawma, Thangchhingpuia and Vanzika.[26]

Development and progress of education in the hill areas began by wooing the parents to send their children to school. As in Ukhrul district, here too most of the parents had an indifferent attitude towards modern education they did not understand its purpose or use, (they were mainly cultivators subsisting on agriculture) and developed some suspicion about the intention and purpose of it. Also relevant to the fact that contiguous to western education, the educated individual became a convert to Christianity in most cases, which meant in practice the discarding of one's traditional practices, social habits, morals, culture, customs, and primordial religion. In those days, the need of modern education was not felt as a necessity. Life was simple. Their main preoccupation was to ensure a successful harvest. If they could get sufficient food for one year, they wanted nothing more. Hence, they were very much preoccupied with their daily work, toiling from dawn to dusk in the field every day, its daily monotony broken by the celebration of many festivals and rituals in which the entire community participated. In such circumstances, it was necessary to utilize the entire family's labour, and education was not a reason to abstain from work. They could not grasp the benefits that would result from modern education and looked askance at it, believing that it would not enable the beneficiary to earn a living. Due to their indifference the expression became common place: "No need of learning idleness," "Failing to learn the way of efficient working in time, you will be simply trailing behind your contemporaries in efficiency and it would become difficult to catch up with your friends in future", etc.[27] These sayings illustrate that education far from empowering the individual, would in fact diminish him/her.

It became necessary to change this attitude of parents and family elders or else the effort to educate the tribals would end in failure. The government and the Missions adopted pro-active measures to get students admitted in their schools by coaxing/convincing the parents, by giving them financial incentives, sometimes in terms of materials like milk powder, clothing, not to speak of the distribution of writing materials, exercise books, pencils, ink, pens, textbooks, etc. In spite of all these efforts and incentives, the attendance of children in school remained minimal.[28]

The impact of Education in the hill areas have to be studied in two geographical zones – 1. the Naga inhabited area comprising of the present four districts of Tamenglong, Senapati including the Sadar Hills, Ukhrul and Chandel and 2.

Chin-Kuki-Mizo or Zomi inhabited area comprising of the present Churachandpur District.[28]

1. NAGA INHABITED AREA

The seed of Modern education were first sowed among the Nagas primarily through Rev. Pettigrew, Government Schools followed and in the decade following Manipur's merger with the Indian Union a number of private schools sprang up-initially only different denominations of Christian missionaries, especially the catholic, set up educational establishment with high levels of academic excellence. They were followed by individuals who set up schools through their own efforts. At the initial stage, it was a herculean task to set up schools, as no parent was willing to send their children to study. Till 1930 there were two Upper Primary Schools in the Naga inhabited areas, one at Mao and another at Ukhrul. After the First World War, their attitude changed and they started demanding schools. Hence, in 1931 another Lower Primary School was opened at Tamenglong.

Pettigrew's initiative was emulated by the American Baptist Mission, who ran one Middle English School at Ukhrul since 1896 but in 1922-23, the school was shifted to at Kangpokpi along with the Mission Headquarters and in 1928-29 it was upgraded to Class VI.

2. EDUCATION IN THE KUKI-CHIN INHABITED AREA

The Hill people inhabiting the Churachandpur district have been known by various nomenclatures like Chin, Kuki, Mizo, and Zomi comprising of the following tribes: (a) Paite (b) Gangte (c) Hmar (d) Mizo (Lushai) (e) Simte (f) Vaiphei and

(g) Zo, etc. In this Southern hill of Manipur, the governmental activity in the field of education was extremely negligible in the first quarter of the twentieth century. The first Government Lower Primary School was established after the First World War at Songtal Village in 1920 with Henthuam as one of the students. As a result of the policy of the government, 'One Teacher-School', the Songtal Lower Primary School was established with the admission of one student Henthuam Tawmbing, and the school subsequently came to be known as the 'Henthuam School'. After him the first batch of students, who completed their schooling upto class III level were Vungluai Tonsing, Vialpum Khuptong, Chinpum Guite, Thuamzathang Tawnsing and Ngullauai Tonsing, the second batch of students comprised Khamkhopau Guite, Ngulthawng and Potadul. After 7 years, the school was shifted to Hanship village in 1927 (as there was not enough students) but the move proved unsatisfactory in that and the school remained without students for a pretty long period of time and ultimately, the Government was forced to close it down. In 1928, another Lower Primary School was established by the Government at Dialkhai with Paukhovung as the teacher.[29]

The first Mission School was established at Senvon in 1911 for this hill area. The people believed in the aphorism that, 'Christianity is education and education is Christianity'. The two were inseparable. The Second Mission School was set up in 1915 with Thangvung Guite as the teacher.

Through the Christian Mission's Scholarship Grant, the scope of education was widened and a few Kuki students were chosen to study medicine at Berry White Medical School at Dibrugarh. They were T. C. Tongngul Gangte, LMP Thangzam Gangte, Phaka Hmar, Vungkhothang and few more.[30]

During the first half of the 20th century, the progress in the field of education among the Kukis was disrupted by the political events caused by the First World War. During the War, the British India Government raised compulsory labour corps from the hill people; the order to do so was fiercely opposed by the Kukis, and resulted in a great uprising, which came to be known in the history of Manipur as the 'Kuki Rebellion' (1917-1919). The Kukis being by nature independent did not want to be under another's control least of all the British. This development took place at a time when the animosity to western education was already weakened. Had the rebellion not occurred the pace of education among the Kukis would have accelerated. But the rebellion eventually spread to all the Kukis-Chin occupied area only. By the spring of 1919, the opposition was crushed and the rebel began to surrender; the operations were brought to a close in May, 1919.[31]

THE BEGINNING OF MODERN EDUCATION IN THE HILLS

The period between 1931 to 1949 can be considered as the period of the real beginning of Modern Education in the hills of Manipur for the following reasons: (1) The tribals abandoned their hostility or indifference to education and began to take interest in sending children to school. (2) Local initiative and cooperation became manifest in the venture of establishing schools in many places. (3) The products of the first hill Schools were now in a position to assume the position of teachers, replacing the first teachers who were not native to the hills Some of these indigenous pioneers from amongst the Nagas and Kukis were Thisan Luikham, Miksha Shimray, K. Vareichung, P. Hollei, all Tangkhul Nagas who attended the Ukhrul Mission M. E. School, and were the first batch of students of the institution, they were followed by Tiba Kilong, Longkhobel

Kom, Thonung, Mono Anal of the Kom and Anal tribes who too received education from the Ukhrul M. E. School, and some Kukis viz., Ngulhao Thomsong, Helkhup, Jamkithang Kuki, Tongkham Singsit and Letzavum, students of the first and second batches of the Ukhrul M. E. School. All of them became instrumental in the spread of Modern Education among the masses of their respective communities. The seed of education sown by the missionaries had germinated and resulted, both in progresses in education and in providing opportunities to the native scholars to find employment as teachers. This profession became in course of time a highly respected vocation and great esteem was attached to the status of teachers.

The contribution of the Christian Missions towards the development of education may be traced in three separate accounts of the American Baptist Mission Area, the North East India General Mission (NEIGM), and the Catholic Mission.

1. American Baptist Mission's Activity in Education

During the period under study, i.e. from 1931-49, the American Baptist Mission in Manipur did remarkable work in education. Rev. William Pettigrew, left Manipur in 1933 but his work was continued by Dr. Crozier, Dr. Werelius and Tanquist. Between the academic years 1932-33 Mission education expanded to include 58 Schools-1 M. E. School, 6 U. P. Schools and 51 L. P. Schools. The primary aim was of course dissemination of the Gospel, but to be truly indoctrinated in the new religion, the tribals had first to be educated, and the missionaries and their teacher-cum-evangelists performed their duties with arduous dedication and sacrifice. Because of their sincere efforts, the tribal population became literate and the converted adult tribal Christians cultivated the habit of reading the Bible daily. Their ability to read and write English enabled many of them to play an active role in politics and religion. For example Late R. Suisa, Rishang Keishing, Late Yangmasho Shaiza, R. Ruichumhao, V. Phaitphang, T. Luikham, D. L. Daiho, Teba Kilong, Longkhobel Kom, K. David, Kuithonang, Dr. (Rev.) J. H. Thumrah etc.[32] It created a new class who could avail of new employment opportunities hitherto denied to them because of their ignorance as also isolation in their mountain fastness.(L) Yangmasho Shaiza and Rishang Keishing were the first tribals Chief Minister of Manipur. Beside that Rishang is the longest eldest serving Member of the Rajya Sabha.

2. The Contribution of the North East India General Mission

After getting permission from the Maharajah of Manipur, Sir Churachand Singh, the NEIGM with its Home Board in the United States of America occupied the old Churachandpur in the present Churachandpur District, opening an M. E. School and Dinwiddie Memorial Bible School in 1930. Rev. Paul Rostad and his wife Ella Rostad also arrived at the Mission Headquarters from their previous headquarters, Lakhipur. Others pioneers of the NEIG mission were Late Thangvung, Late Vungkhothang, Taivel, Pumkhothong, Siamkung, Nengzachin, D. Khaizalian, Thawngzathang etc.

The NEIG Mission established and ran 24 schools prior to the Second World War, 1 M. E. School, 23 L. P. schools and one Bible school. At the time the practice of Sunday schools was to teach the Alphabets in Roman script known as 'A, AW, B, CH,' to all present whether young or old, thus enabling even those who had no opportunities to learn: how to read and write. This in turn enabled them to improve their lot in life by practical application of the knowledge gained not only to their daily activities but to raising their standard of living. The progress of education was adversely affected by the Second World War; the staff members in the Headquarters office and School had to flee due to the dangers posed by the Japanese advance and many were recruited as porters. Despite this setback, literacy registered a remarkable increase. Rev. Jamkhothang remarked, "Without the Mission work, the condition of the tribes would have been much, much lower than what it is today. Though not all of them have become Christians, much of their old way of life was given up. Their whole outlook changed. Their living standard became much higher, those who, at one time, were to be coaxed to send their children to schools, were now mad after education." He further observed, the 'Gospel was a marvelous light to the tribes, in spite of their ignorance and superstitions they were attracted to the Gospel. They, who for many years sacrificed animal blood to the devil out of fear, could somehow by the power of the Holy Spirit, understand the sacrifice of Jesus Christ which was out of Love'.[33]

3. Catholic Mission

Because of the attitude of the British colonial administrators, who favoured only Protestant Missionaries and later the Baptists, the Catholic Mission was unable to start work in Manipur till after they left the State.

The First Catholic Missionary, Fr. Ansgar Koenigsbauer, came to Manipur in 1912. He travelled via Dimapur, Kohima, and Mao and reached Imphal. After his arrival at Imphal, Fr. Ansgar Koenigsbauer was received in audience by the Raja several times. He sought for permission to establish a Mission Centre at Imphal, and the Raja had no objections. From the time of their entry into Manipur, the Catholic Missionaries made rapid and continuous progress in the fields of evangelisation, humanitarian works and educational services. They were not content with merely scratching the surface. The arms of the Missionaries stretched out to include every facet of the life of the people. The Missionaries established Churches, Schools, boarding houses and dispensaries for the material and moral welfare of the people. There is no doubt that Catholic education has reached into the far interior of Manipur into places as distant from one another as for example Chingjaroi (1980), Churachandpur (1968), Hundung (1965), Imphal (North, 1957), Imphal (Suoth, 1975), Nungbi (1975), Punanmei (Mao, 1969) Singngat (1978), Sugnu (1965), Tamenglong (1972), Ukhrul (1978) etc.[34]

Of the Christian Missionaries who came to Manipur, the Catholics were the most recent in the field, and yet it is they alone who have left their stamp on education in Manipur and brought or increased the level of literacy in areas where it was non-existent or negligible. Although few in number, the Catholics have done more than any other missionaries in Manipur. A large number of people educated in the Catholic Institutions are holding responsible jobs, or are engaged in some form or other of activity that has improved their lot. The educated persons naturally seek higher grades of employment, which in turn brings a steady rise in standard of living. The Missionaries have succeeded in modernising the tribal people of Manipur. Indeed, they have unlocked and opened their minds to a new world view and value system. There are now many bright Scientists, Professors, Doctors, Engineers, Politicians etc. among the tribal Christian Communities in Manipur. Quite naturally, the emergence of this new professional class in a traditional agrarian society has led to the emergence of a middle class in the formerly egalitarian tribal society.

Education undoubtedly was a single, most important factor which modernized the tribal, lifting them from the old world to the new. Not only did education open new doors, it introduced them to a global culture with all its attendant ramifications. It altered the structured of society and raised the standard of living. It brought literacy to a society, which had been illiterate, it enhanced personal development and growth, providing job opportunities in sectors to which the tribals had never aspired, it brought them into the folds of a major world religion which enabled them to establish close links with Church goers all over the world. But above all, education set the tribal on the path of progress and development, and because of their early start in education they achieved an enviable proficiency in the English language which stood them in good stead when they applied for jobs or appeared for competitive exams as for e.g. The UPSC examinations, UGC, NET, etc.

IMPACT OF MODERN EDUCATION

The effectiveness of education as a means for attaining their ends was well realized by the Christian Mission Societies. Literary and education were necessary to read and understand the word of God, which was integral to the Protestant understanding of evangelism. The need for Catechesis or instrument in Christian faith, Church leaders, teachers, social acceptance, etc., was some of the motives for Christian educational efforts.[35] Likewise the chief motive behind the missionaries' educational endeavors was the propagation of the Christian faith. As such in the early years of the missionaries' enterprises among the tribals, education became an inseparable part of their evangelistic work. They went hand in hand. Therefore, any study on the impact of education on the hill tribes in the early years would always be linked with that of Christianity.

The tribes of Manipur owe their gratitude to the pioneer Christian Missionaries for bringing modern education and its consequent benefits. Though formal education was first introduced among the Tangkhul Nagas by William Pettigrew, who was given all authority in this field by the state machinery, it would be wrong to dismiss the hill tribes as having no education system prior to their contact with the Christian missionaries. No human society exists and grows without education of some kind. The tribal society though without the formal schooling of the west, regarded education as operative at all stages of human life and very much in the interest of the cohesion of the village community.[36]

In the old days, the most important institution, which served as an educational centre was the Morung/Zawlbuk or bachelor's dormitory. In the absence of any institutionalized system of schooling the bachelor dormitory played the foremost part in making them responsible members of society, emphasis was on vocational crafts which when put in practical use would bring in income to supplement that coming from agriculture. They learnt the arts of handicrafts like wood making, cane and bamboo works, black smithy, etc., whereas womenfolk learnt and did different kinds of cloth making, arts and embroidery works during their stay in the dormitory.[37] Much of the tribal culture, its customs and traditions has been transmitted from generation to generation through the media of folk music and dance, folktales and oral historical traditions, carving of figures on stone and wood, and designs on clothes. And the centre where all these teaching and learning process were carried out was the men's dormitories.[38] But ironically, among the Kuki-Chins, there were no women dormitories.

However, the traditional dormitory system did not prove sufficient when the new education system was introduced. Education being one of the most important agencies for bringing change in any individual or society, the modern education system on the western model as introduced by Rev. Pettigrew, to a large extent shaped the new tribal society that emerged after the coming to Christianity in Manipur. More than Christianity, it was the introduction of formal education through establishment of schools and its related developments; that brought a great change to the Morung/Dormitory way of living. The children spent their time in the Schools rather than the dormitories and the School became central to their lives. With the passage of time, many youngsters left their ancestral villages to pursue higher studies outside, first in the State and then outside of it. The Morung was no longer regarded as an essential institution, which changed girls and boys into responsible women and men. The focus now centred on modern education and in the changed environment the Morung/Zawlbuk or Bachelor dormitories lost much of its relevance and ultimately died a natural death.

Modern education together with Christianity opened a whole new world to the hill tribes of Manipur. One of the impacts of the new education system was in undermining their superstitious beliefs and ideas. The early missionaries demanded not only change of hearts, but also change in their way of living. They soon learnt that the Gospel contradicted their superstitions and belief in imaginary spirits. (Religious rites and rituals were meant for appeasing the anger of the evil spirits whom they consider responsible for sickness and failure of crops). The Institutions of Schools effected revolutionary changes in their ways of life. The educated imbibed new morals, values and world view, not only because of the content of the curriculum but also because education exposed the hill tribes to different people and cultures and brought them out of their isolated geographical and cultural pockets. They began to travel, to interact with others and consciously or unconsciously modeled themselves on the pattern of others outside their tribe. Exposure to a new world with different economic administrative, political, social structures, different politics and philosophies and forms of government, it new educational and social institutions were bound to alter the world view of the tribal people. The new world view that they encountered also brought about a change in their way of thinking as well as living. The introduction of modern education succeeded in raising the socio-economic status of the tribal people.

A significant impact of modern formal education was seen in occupational changes among the tribals. Their traditional occupation had been agriculture, which required continuing inputs of manual labour. However, with the spread of education new employment opportunities were introduced. The creation of salaried posts was something new to the people. More and more people opted for government Jobs, which were found to be more lucrative, in addition to providing security as also social prestige. At the same time, the salary enabled them to lead more comfortable lives and appreciably raised their standard of living. For the first time they enjoyed some disposable income. Besides government jobs, they found employment as teachers, catechists, pastors, priests deacons, social workers etc. and later on in specialized disciplines like medicine, engineering, accountancy, etc. Simultaneously, their induction into new employment opportunities gave birth in course of time to what may be termed as a 'middle class' in tribal society. This emerging middle class possessed the knowledge and skills to take advantage of emerging opportunities to better themselves and to enhance their social standing. This enabled them to become the religious and public leaders of their own community.

They were now in a position to implement or experiment with new ideas, technology, beliefs, means of governance, structure of institutions etc. And since they enjoyed the distinction of being educated, their words had more weight than that of their fellowmen who remained illiterate.

Education also helped and paved the way for the hill tribes to attain a higher standard of living. There was a marked improvement in the quality of their life. Adoption of hygienic ways of living, proper dietary habits, medical care and medical services, all contributed to a better life. The missionaries' teachings were not confined to the Gospel and the three 'R's, but extended to all aspects of tribal life. For instance in the Schools and boarding institutions children were taught hygienic habits through practical training in cleanliness. They were taught what constituted respectable dress with an emphasis on neatness and cleanliness. They were taught the necessity of bathing and washing their clothes regularly. This was different to their age-old practices and traditions. A change in house planning and construction followed. A notable contribution in this area was made by Rev. U. M. Fox who introduced carpentry into the hills and trained the simple village people to make modern furniture and build more comfortable and practical houses.

Since the new houses were constructed of more durable materials they were better able to withstand the ravages of time, especially strong winds and storms which often blew off the roofs of houses.

Not only the tribals but the State machinery also benefitted from Rev. Pettigrew's educational efforts. To cite a few examples; in the early period, when the govt. decided to carry out the first real census of the Tangkhul Naga tribe in 1911, it had no have lack of personnel in the form of enumerators. Enumerators were appointed from among the teachers and higher-class scholars of the Ukhrul Station School. As most of them were Tangkhuls themselves, work could proceed smoothly and satisfactorily. They possessed the added advantage of knowing both the areas and its inhabitants. The same task was entrusted to the missionary and his students during the 1921 census operation. The Ukhrul station School served both as a secular and religious training centre when the hill country was divided into sections or areas for administrative efficiency with direct official supervision at close quarters, all the human service posts required were filled up by those who had been wholly or in part educated at this school.

One of the negative impacts of modern education and Christianity, for instance new converts in haste started looking askance and abandoning their traditional practices customs and religion. In the process great damage was done to the preservation of folklore, oral traditions, songs, and dances etc., which were the means to transmit the rich culture of the tribals from one generation to the next.

It is an undeniable fact that western education and Christianity hastened the pace of progress and modernization among the hill people. There is truth in the remark that without necessary efforts at providing education, the ethnic groups of this region would have been lagging behind and at the mercy of the more advanced group from mainland India.[39] Education opened a world of opportunities to the tribals and brought about a remarkable change in their mental outlook. It is found that the tribes or communities which first came into contact with Christianity and western education were more advanced and progressed faster than the others. Among the Nagas in Nagaland, the Aos having had the opportunity of being the first to acquire modern education through the efforts of the Baptists Missionary showed remarkable progress as compared to the other tribes.[40]

In the case of Manipur hills, it was the Tangkhul Nagas who first came into contact with modern education through the Missionary Rev. Pettigrew. The first School was opened at Ukhrul, the land of the Tangkhuls and for years, it was the only well maintained school that catered to the educational needs of the hill tribes. It served as a training ground for future leaders. In fact, whole generations of religious and secular leaders were trained here. Though students from other tribes attended this school, majority of the students were from the Tangkhul tribe. And education being the harbinger of progress among the hill tribes it is not surprising that the Tangkhuls made great progress and were found to be more advanced and modernized than the other communities in the early years. The communities of North East India once awakened to themselves by the new world view provided by the Christian message and assisted by education, have proved to be the most progressive-minded on the whole sub-continent. In a matter of a couple of generations, they are catching up with the most advanced societies.[41]

For the hill tribes of Manipur education was the chief means of enlightenment. It helped them to acquire new ideas. Old beliefs, ways and concepts yielded place to new ones as modern education posed a challenge to many of the blind beliefs and faiths of the tribals. It had an impact on the way of thinking and broadened the mental horizon of the tribal. Earlier their world was confined to their village. Education exposed the tribals to the outside world and made them more curious to learn and know the happenings in the outside world. After the introduction of modern education, the momentum of change and progress among the tribes has been extraordinary. Here we may quote F. S. Downs who said that 'The impact of modern education was likely to be greater on a people with a relatively unsophisticated background and with no literary traditions'.[42]

The beginning of education of women was a major breakthrough in the transformation of society. In the days when education of girls was practically unheard of and was strongly opposed, Mrs. Alice Pettigrew took on the challenge of providing some sort of education to the Tangkhul girls at Ukhrul. It was through her relentless efforts that gradually interest in girls' education was aroused and together with her husband, she with devotion, sacrifice and love began and carried on the education of women. The attitude of parents and society towards women's education changed greatly, women's education was no longer envisaged as an exercise in futility but as a path leading to empowerment and development and soon in many families no distinction was made between the boys and girls with reference to education.

One of the consequences of this education was a gradual disenchantment with traditional vocations such as weaving and kitchen gardening. Moreover studies and focused trainings in new vocations, left little time to pursue these traditional crafts, even if the girls/women were so inclined. In the long term because of the transference of educated women to new professions, some designs and other crafts and handiwork of the tribes became extinct or nearly so, because the educated girls preferred to attire themselves in western clothes, which they viewed as better, grander and more respectable than their traditional dress. No doubt it is human nature to be attracted to something 'new and novel'. In the first flush of their enthusiasm, they inflicted considerable damage to their traditional past-times, but fortunately, in recent times there has been a resurgence of traditional crafts and designs.

There is hardly any difference of opinion among writers on the positive role the Christian Missionaries played in the growth and development of the languages and literature of the region. Before the advent of the missionaries, the tribals were illiterate and without a written language. The reduction of the tribal language in the Roman Script has had far reaching benefits.

REFERENCES

1. Karotemprel Sebastian, 'The Impact of Christianity on the tribes of North East India' *in the 'Tribal situation in North East India'*, Edited by Sarthak Sengupta, Inter India Publication, New Delhi, 1994. p. 136.
2. Irene Salam, 'Catholic Mission Education in Manipur.' A published thesis submitted to Manipur University for the degree of Philosophy, 1987. p. 202.
3. Jamini Devi, *Education in Manipur*, Imphal, 1989. p. 54.
4. Basanta, N., *Socio-Economic Change in Manipur 1891-1947*, Imphal, 1998. p. 34.
5. Jeyaseelan, L., *Impact of Missionary Movement in Manipur*, New Delhi. p. 159.
6. "Reverend William Pettigrew and Modern Education in Manipur", L. Leiren Singh in Pettigrew Centenary Celebrations Committee Manipur, 1996. p. 8.
7. Luikham, T., *Short History of the Manipur Baptist Christian*, Calcutta, *1984*. pp. 7-12.
9. Jeyaseelan, L., *Impact of Missionary Movement in Manipur*, Scholar Publishing House, Delhi, 1996. p. 161.
10. Lien, Z. Z., *The U-Now People*, Churachandpur, 1981, pp. 118-119.
11. Jeyaseelan. L., *op. cit.* p. 161.
12. Lal Dena, *Christian Missions and Colonialism*, Shillong, 1988. p. 35.
13. Lolly, R. R., *The Baptist Church in Manipur*, Imphal, 1985. p. 43.
14. Lal Dena. *op. cit.* p. 92.
15. Lolly, *op. cit.* p. 23.

16. Administrative Report of the Manipur Political Agency 1897-98, p. 4.
17. Basanta, N., *Socio-economic Change in Manipur 1891-1947*, Imphal, 1998. p. 88.
18. *Ibid.* p. 90.
19. Lolly, *op. cit.* pp. 32-33.
20. *Ibid.*
21. Champhang, J., *Christian Life in a Tribal Context in Manipur*, Ukhrul, 1990. p. 26.
22. Basanta, N. *op. cit.* p. 91.
23. *Ibid.*
24. Administrative Report of the Manipur Political Agency, 1937-38. p. 26.
25. Khaizalian, D., *Taangthupha Tunma leh Tunung*, published at Lamka, 1986. p. 74.
26. Guite, P. K., 'Development of Education in the Hill Areas of Manipur'. Unpublished Ph.D thesis, Manipur University, 1991, p. 227.
27. *Ibid.*
28. There are nine districts in Manipur, four districts are in the valley and five districts are in the Hills.
29. Songtal Village Souvenir, Churachandpur (1902-88). p. 26.
30. Khaizalian, D., *Taangthupha Tunma leh Tunung, op. cit.* p. 102.
31. Shakespeare, Major J., *History of Assam Rifles*, Cultural Publishing House, 1922. p. 236.
32. *Ibid.*
33. Guite, P. K., *op. cit.* p. 232.
34. Jamkhothang, Rev. T., 'A proposed Guidance of the North East India General Mission on Schoo'. An unpublished Bachelor of Divinity thesis, Serampore Theological College, 1963. p. 70.
35. Salam, Irene, *Catholic Education in Manipur*, New Delhi, 1989. p. 90.

36. Dr. Sebastian Kartemprel, *op. cit.* p. 35.
37. Shishak, Reverend (Dr.) Tuisem A., 'Nagas and Education', in Nagas at Work, NSUD Publication, New Delhi, 1996. pp. 29-30.
38. Khashim, Ruivah, *Social Change among the Nagas (Tangkhuls)*, Cosmo Publication, Delhi, 1993. p. 216.
39. Shimray, Ayai, 'Revd. William Pettigrew and His Times 1869-1943'. Unpublished Ph.D. thesis submitted to Manipur University, 2006, p. 214
40. Khashim, Ruivah, 1993. *op. cit.* p. 21.
41. Patricia, Mukhim, 'Christian Impact on North East India and National Integration' in J. Puthenpurakal (Ed.), *Impact of Christianity on North East India*, Vendrame Institute Publications, Shillong, 1996. p. 66.
42. Shimray, Ayai, 2006. *op. cit.* p. 219.
43. *Ibid.* p. 219.

Four

The Emergence of the Middle Class Assertion of Ethnic Identity

One perhaps inadvertent effect of Christianity and western education coupled with colonial rule was the emergence of a middle class in tribal society, which altered the balance of power. There is no evidence to prove that one of the aims of the above was to alter social structure, or facilitate the rise of a new class. Moreover, this new middle class did not fit the classic Marxist description of a middle class. It owed its advantages to the benefits directly or indirectly derived from Christianity and western education.

This new middle class subtly but inevitably changed the balance of power in tribal society. By virtue of modern education they dominated positions in almost all vocations- be it administration, education, governance, media, technology, medicine, pastoral vocations, entrepreneurship etc. In the altered landscape, it was this middle class, which basically sprang up from the lower rungs of the social order, despite the fact that tribal society is by and large egalitarian which began to assume the reins of political leadership, gradually rendering the position and responsibilities of traditional chiefs' non-essential. Simultaneously they became the models of social etiquette and also trend setters- in whatever they did, the manner in which they talked, ate, dressed, functioned, they were emulated by their tribes and community-in fact their behavior became a benchmark with which to adjudge other members of the community. Moreover, the altered world view and perceptions of the middle class, although not undermining traditional values, beliefs and practices, has introduced new values, beliefs, institutions which have enabled the tribals to come out of isolation, and to imbibe a more open culture which enables them to combine the best of the new, with the abiding values of the old. Power to influence and control lies with the middle class.

Tribal society is distinct from other sections in terms of its socio-economic and political backwardness. Therefore, the process of economic and political development is very negligible. In fact, in the face of change, the socio-economic and political outlook of the tribals has undergone tremendous sea change. Being sandwiched between the traditional forms, hereditary institutions, and modern representative system of the democratic system, the tribals in Manipur have been in a predicament and precarious stalemate. More so while tracing the growth and role of the middle class and their ethnic assertion among the hill tribes of Manipur.

In the 19th and early 20th century, a diverse range of discourse debated the identity and existence of a new middle class that emerged in North east India and among the hill tribes of Manipur. (viz., The Kukis and the Nagas).

Since it had been observed that there was an absence of middle class among the Hill tribes prior to the colonial Rule, it is necessary to study briefly the traditional customary system and structure that existed among this two hill tribes of Manipur. To trace the emergence and growth of the Middle class among the

Hill Tribes a look at the nature of the pre-colonial rule, colonial and administrative changes introduced during the British rule, the coming of Christianity and their evangelizing process and the post-Independence period, will give a clear concept of the emergence of the middle class. The role of the new middle class, and the impact on the tribal society, their perception of identity and nationalism, which will have great ramification in the socio-political events that ensued in the post-Independence Period.

In the late 19th and early 20th century, few studies were made on the identity and practices of these emerging new middle class that emerged in the colonial period. The rise of the new middle class is marked by a long historical trajectory that is cemented by the coming of Christianity and the education introduced by the Christian missionaries as part of their evangelizing process. As Leela Fernandes remarked, 'An analysis of the historical roots of the new middle class demonstrates the continuity between earlier periods and trend in the post independence period, and allows us to specify the particular characteristic of the new middle class that are associated with the contemporary politics of economic liberalization.' She further contended three characteristics, which stands out with regard to the rise of the new middle class in the colonial period,

'First, the distinctiveness of this social group is marked by specific kinds of socio-economic resources such as access to English education and modern education forms of professional employment. These resources came to distinguish this social group from traditional elites, and led to specific forms of connection with and dependence on the colonial states.

Second, the newness of this middle class rested on an emerging set of political claims of public representatives that this group made within the realms of democratic civic life. The political assertiveness of this new middle class rested on its claim to represent the general interests of the public, often against colonial state power.

Finally, this claim of representation was continually accompanied by a projection of self-identification that was marked by a politics of destruction from both the colonial debate and more marginalized section social group.[1]

In view of the above characterization, the emergence of the new middle class among the tribes in Manipur was the education of a few converted local Christians, which was unprecedented in the growth of national Identity. Roy Burman devised the term 'sub-nationalism' which was validated by Chaube, according to him the 'the unequal development of the hills and plain areas accentuates this movement. The middle class among the tribals are the leaders of the sub-national movement and they want equality of opportunity in respect of employment and consequently of political status. As Comte opined 'the evolution of intellect determines the main course of social evolution' so also the establishment of mission schools and emergence of educated few shape the rise of Middle class and their subsequent awareness of identifying to certain identity based on tribe, clans, language and culture.[2]

Hence, given the complexity surrounding the hill tribes of Manipur in relation to colonial administration, Christianity and education, a brief study of the hill tribes will highlight the emergence of the middle class and the assertion of their identity base on ethnic lines.

TRIBAL HISTORICAL BACKGROUND

Manipur is geographically divided into hills and valleys. The Five hill districts constitute 90 per cent of Manipur area and accounts for 38 per cent of the population. The hills are home to

33 scheduled tribes as well as other minor tribes. Historically, Manipur was under independent monarchical system of governance. The Kuki and Naga are the main hill tribes of Manipur, listed as scheduled tribes under the Indian constitution. The Kukis living in Nagaland, Assam, Tripura and Manipur have closer cultural, traditional and ethnic affinity with the people of Mizoram, Chittagong Hills of Bangladesh and the Chins of the Chin Hills in Burma rather than with their neighbors. The same holds good for the Nagas. Despite conspicuous nature at the height of diversity in ethnicity, culture, tradition, language, their peculiar emotional upsurge they integrate themselves burying their hatchet of age-old age war of attrition, under the nomenclature of 'Naga' and a language called 'Nagamese'. These encouraged them to demand for a separate state for Nagaland which eventually materialized and later a demand for integration of the 'Nagas' of Manipur into greater Nagaland.[3] They are Jhum cultivators but as they have comparatively little land, they are compelled to husband their resources. They are unable to shift their fields from year to year, so they cut an elaborate system of drainage along the face of the hill, and thus checked to some extent the tendency of the rainwater to carry off the surface soil.[4] Every village has three hereditary officers, namely Khulakpa, Lup-lakpa and Lampu, any officers beside these are elected. The authority of the village chief they have rejected, but each village has become a small republic, the safety of which, experience have taught the members, is only to be gained by strictly observing the rights of person and property.[5] The Government of every Naga is a purely democratically one, and whenever anything of public importance has to be undertaken, all the chiefs (both old and young) meet together in solemn conclave, and then discuss and decide the action to be taken, and even then it often happens that the minority will not be bound by either the wish or act of

the majority;and as to any one single chief exercising absolute control over his people, the thing is unheard of.[6]

Traditionally, the village is the highest political unit among the Kukis, and chief of the villages and his council of Ministers who function within a territorial Jurisdiction, wield political authority and prerogatives over the villages in the form of absolute political power.[7] The Kukis practiced jhum Cultivation. Partial terrace cultivation too is practiced.[8] Though many have tried to draw a similarity between the Haosa and the zamindar and often jump to the conclusion that the Haosa (Chief) was a despot and tyrannical in nature. However, there are certain provisions, such as liberty to leave the village at will, if the Haosa fails to protect the interest of the villagers; his power as chief depends upon the people. Hence among the Kuki society, their exist two class of people, the Chief and his council of ministers, and the gentry, existence of middle class is absent. Trade and manufacture among the hill-men was practically non-existent. Trade is confined, so far as Manipur is concerned, almost entirely to the bartering of raw cotton and a few articles in the bazaar; salt is chiefly taken in return. The hill-men also for the most part supply the valley with the firewood required for the inhabitants. Iron is procured from Kachar and Manipur, and manufactured into daos and spear heads.[9]

COLONIAL ADMINISTRATION

The British East India Company first came as traders, then as missionaries, as rulers, in limited contact with the indigenous population. However, after they came, they felt the need for a more secure context in which to live and work. This led to the establishment of a colonial administration, which would make possible the various kinds of economic exploitation and cultural aggrandization they deemed necessary. Thus was born a modern colony, a political unit under the sovereignty of British power, which assured law and order within its bounds. Colonial rule also meant colonial administration. Hence, the traditional ruler was no longer the ultimate authority.[10] In Manipur too, after the Anglo-Manipur war of 1891 Manipur, a princely independent monarchical state was brought under colonial rule. Colonial administration was introduced in the Hill and the valley. New Strata of classes emerged to take the place of the old. In the colonial situation, money and education have been the major leverage.[11] The assumption of authority by Raja Churachand Singh on 15th may 1907 was of significance in the annals of the History of modern Manipur. According to arrangements made for the state, the Raja was the President and the Vice-President, an I.C.S. Officer from Assam. The President was given the charge of education, medical, and armed state police, and the vice-president, hill tribes, finance and revenue of all kinds (i.e. besides land revenue). A point of fundamental significance which marked British policy towards the hill tribes was the recognition of the tribal chiefs who, no doubt enjoyed considerable power and privileges within their chiefdoms. Their main concern was to collect hill house tax and exact forced labour (pothang) through the tribal chiefs.[12] The contact between the hill people and the British administrator was made through an official known as 'Lambu'. In the pre-colonial period, they were not more than a peon, acting as interpreter between the Chiefs and the Raja. However, their position changed during the Colonial period, they were given a dual role-as interpreter and an advisory role on matters pertaining to hill areas. Their position was greatly elevated as the British officials depended much more on the Lambus rather than, the chief. Thus the Lambus, who tried to exert and increase their influence and power over the hill areas, superseded the position of the Chief. They always overruled the judgments of the Chiefs and enjoyed special treatment in every way.[13]

The Hill administration was divided into five divisions, each division under one Lam Subedar under whose supervision seven Lambus were appointed for the administration of the hill area. A Lambu was originally a Meitei official who dealt with rural administration. During the political control of the Maharaja of Manipur, the Lambus who were not appointed officially by the state roamed the hills as brokers between the state official and the villages in respect of service under Lallup system. They were oppressive to the hill tribes in their dealings. However, after the colonial rule these Lambus were appointed and paid salaries, seven rupees originally. The Lam Subedar was also paid a salary. The Lambus in the hills were appointed from influential tribal families in the villages. They became corrupt and oppressive and became powerful petty officials of the colonial rule. They performed multifarious duties for the government.[14]

Hence, the colonial administration created a situation for the process of modernisation that touched every facet of tribal life-political, social, economic and cultural. Some of the more important changes brought about by British administration were: the subjection of the tribes to an introduction of an alien administrative and judicial system and the imposition of a entirely new principles of authority and jurisprudence; the introduction of money economy and consumer goods such as mill cloth and kerosene lanterns which undermined the largely self-sufficient economies of the tribes and created a new concept of wealth; the development of modern education, bringing in a number of outsiders administrators, clerks, soldiers, merchants technicians and missionaries, who provided new life style model particularly in the town area that grew up around the administrative centres; and the imposition of laws that seriously affected traditional institutions. Rise of a new class of people who wielded much power than the chiefs, and undermined the authority of the Chiefs. It created a new social order where the Lambus acted as a privileged class, changing the old tribal social order whence the chief no longer wielded much influence. Relatively, the Lambus acted as superiors to the chief.

EMERGENCE AND ROLE OF MIDDLE CLASS

The emergence of a middle class among the tribals of Manipur is associated with the growth of Christianity, colonial administration, urbanization, money economy and the Tribal officials employed in the colonial administration. Since Christianity is synonymous with education, those who became Christians were automatically provided with modern education with English as the medium of instruction. Broadly, speaking two classes emerged – a class of literate Christians and a class of non-conformist illiterate traditionalists. Henceforth the literate Christian, comprising basically of the religious leaders represented the elites, and the non-traditionalist elites comprised of Chiefs and heads of a village administration. As a consequence of the colonial hegemony, colonial administration was introduced throughout the hills of Manipur. The introduction of a new administrative policy destabilized the traditional social tribal polity of the hills. Combined with this the influx of Christian missionaries under the Baptist, Welsh Mission, Seventh Day Adventist and the Roman Catholic among the hills of Manipur contributed to the further disintegration of the Tribal traditional social set up. It ended an old era and ushered in the dawn of a new era of breaking from the past. Christian missionaries forbade head hunting, worship of natural deities, spirits etc, slavery, inter-tribal warfare and feuds, various institutions like the bachelor's dormitory and cultural celebrations. Though some semblance of the traditional socio-cultural practices were still retained the link between the old and the new was strained and ultimately transformed. The colonial policy throughout the period under study has been to consistently legitimize and uphold the authority of the traditional chiefs, whereas the missionary work, basing on the theory of cultural selectivity, contributed to the disruption of the traditional society. Inevitably, tension arose between the traditional elites and the emerging elites. While the traditional elites rallied behind the officials, the modern elites rallied behind the missionaries. Obviously, the loyalty of the new elites to the traditional authority became gradually loosened and the chiefs rightly saw in them a potential danger.

As Christianity made its inroad among the hill people of Manipur, they were imparted western education, although as a process to evangelization, it created a new class of people, which may be referred to as the Middle class elites. These new class of people educated in Mission schools superseded the Chiefs and the elders. Eventually the educated new converts took the initiating role first in evangelizing the non Christian brethren, later they assumed much more important positions not only in the Church but also in the society, taking up the mantle of leadership in guiding the people not only in matters pertaining to daily life, but to society, polity and economy as a whole.

Meanwhile the colonial administrative policy of the British added to the stature and authority of the 'Lambus' who acted and imitated the colonial officials as a new class of people among the hill tribes. The 'Lambus' position and prestige began to grow as the Vice-President consulted them in all administrative policy concerning the hills of Manipur. Educated young men upto primary level of education were appointed as Lambus, although they were mere peons and translators. Due to the overburdening of the Vice-president with multifarious responsibilities in looking after the hill administration, the

Lambus were able to exert much influence upon the hill people and acted as small petty officials during the colonial period. There was no way of circumventing this petty officer, who demanded some form of recognition and subservience from the tribals. Matters came to such a pass that they assumed that they were entitled to special prerogatives. Accustomed as they were to their own life of independence, the chiefs of the Kuki especially, who acted as sovereigns over their hill domain and villages resented deeply the power the Lambus exercised over them. They felt that the Lambus, who were not more than peons in the pre-British period, treated them as subordinate. Therefore for the Kuki Chiefs, who always maintained an equal status with the King of Manipur, this idea of Lambus superiority was not acceptable or palatable. On the other hand, Lambus took advantage of their new position, and always overruled the judgment of chiefs in cases pertaining to the village or tribe. They demanded special treatment in every village. At the same time these people despite being representatives of the British authorities over the Hill areas, never cared to effect any improvement in the hill areas. Instead of this, they used to take money to settle/adjucate case and indulged in different forms of corruption. Kuki Chiefs traditional entitlement to taxes and tributes from the villagers and their slaves, such as payment of saleng (Portion of meat hind leg) Salu (head of the killed game), Changseo (payment of fixed basket-full of paddy annually) could no longer be enjoyed, the people gradually declined to make such payments in lieu they paid taxes to the Colonial officials such as land revenue, hill tax which was collected by the Lambus. The ties that bound the chiefs and the villagers gradually eroded and the chief's position as leader of his people was severely compromised. The British policy of appointing educated people (basically primary education) converted to Christianity as Lambus, schoolteachers, peons and police constables paved the way for the growth of a new social class which hitherto had never existed in the pre-colonial period.

In recognising the authority of the tribal chiefs the colonial administrators kept in mind their primary interest of using the chiefs to collect taxes and ensure that forced labour (pothang) was available for the purpose of carrying the baggage of touring officials, arranging food and proper lodging etc. Pothang was of two kinds- pothang bekari and pothang senkhai. According to pothang bekari, the people were forced to carry wily-nilly the goods, luggages or sometimes the touring officials in a palanquin. While under the pothang senkhai, each household in a village was to subscribe money or sometimes chicken, eggs, etc.[15] Since these oppressive policies were to be enforced through the chiefs of the villages, the British gave red blankets to the Chiefs as a symbol of their status in the hill districts.[16]

The British in order to consolidate their hold over Manipur's hills appointed the educated young men among the hill tribes as school teachers, medical practitioners, compounders, and vaccinators. Lonkhobel Kom, the first convert into Christianity among the Kukis was appointed as second clerk in the sub-divisional office of the south west area, Teba Kilong another convert was the head clerk in the sub-divisional office in Ukhrul, beside Seijalut brought up in the Ukhrul school and later a teacher at the new secondary school at Kangpokpi was also the third clerk in the same office at Ukhrul. Among the Nagas Levi, a clerk represented the Zemei and Liangmais in the Memorandum to the Simon Commission in 1929 when a committee visited Kohima.

The most significant change brought by the colonial economy was monetization of the tribal economy. Trade among the hills had already existed in the pre-colonial period through barter system. Prior to the advent of the colonial rule, the hill people did not use currency, though the currency 'sel' was widely used in Imphal valley. It was used in very limited numbers. Imposition of hill house taxes, payment of salaries to the hill communities employed under the colonial government and by the missionaries, created the importance of money economy. It prompted a desire to be absorbed into government service; this new class of people, did all they could to get education as a leverage to securing economic benefits.

A striking and remarkable role played by the educated converts, of missionary schools was evangelization and growth of denominational Christian Churches. Sharing the same religion as the colonial rulers, they developed an allegiance to the British rule. As such during the First World War when the British raised a labours corps, it was these early converts who convinced the people to volunteer, while on the other hand it was the belief of the colonial rulers that Christianity and education would improve the material condition of the Indian people including the hill people of Manipur. According to Lal Dena, such a policy was beneficial for the extension of their missionary work. The missionaries also emphasised that such help would enable the fostering of a closer relationship between the rulers and the ruled, and would be of advantage to both.

Thus because of the presence of few but influential pro-missionary officials, the company was thus made to think that the introduction of Christianity and evangelisation was to the governments advantage. As such, William Pettigrew, the first missionary who came to Manipur was appointed the Superintendent of the first real census of the Hills. In view of his success in raising the Manipur Labour Corps, which consisted of 2000 men, of whom 1200 were from Tangkhul Nagas amongst whom Pettigrew had been working for the last 20 years, the British Army awarded him The Kaiser-i-Hind silver medal and war medal in recognition of his distinguished public and military service during the war Period. Interestingly the Christian Kukis sided with the government and acted as the means of influencing the non Christian Kukis to volunteer for the war service. In fact, one Kuki Evangelist, Ngulhao mobilized as many as 500 non-Christians Kukis for the Labour Corps. In consideration of the contribution made by the missionaries and the native Christians towards the global war and the Kuki Punitive Measures, (Representing the neutral party of the Kuki uprising, of 1917 to 1919) the state government had thus granted a land for the mission Headquarters at Kangpokpi on the Imphal–Dimapur road.[17] For the second labour Corps 817 was raised including 60 Kukis and Zeme (from Berema and Henima). They were not sent to France but, were mobilized to suppress the Kuki rebellion.[18] When the Anglo-Kuki War broke out in 1917 the Christian Kukis refrained from participating. Rather they sided with the British. More so it was the Christian Kukis who were recruited in the Labour corps to fight in France. Letkholal Singson, son of the chief of Kangjang and Onkai Sitlhou, chief of Songdo who were on good terms with the British persuaded, the chief of Sangnao to surrender.[19]

Inevitably, tension rose between the traditionalist elite and emerging middle class elite. The newly educated middle class elite looked up to the European as models of behaviour and tended to become pro-western in their attitudes. They also began to regard themselves as belonging to more or less different categories and assumed new leadership-political and religious. In fact, tension arose between the traditional leaders who upheld the existing institutions and practices and the middle class elites favoring the western values and democratic practices. The hill people became exposed to the new western ideas arriving in the wake of missionary activities, Christianity and education. The emerging middle class tended to be more and more vocal in their attack against the traditional rights and privileges of the chiefs. The moment the new converts became

Christian, they abandoned their traditional hairstyle, wore European dresses and received patronage from the colonial administrators in the form of employment in the state administration and the missions, receiving a cash salary. This elevated them to a new social stature. Moreover, their cash salary enabled them to dominate the economic outlook because for so long the hill people only knew a barter economy. New possession of money gave them a feeling of power, an air of pre-eminence over the people. The new middle class eventually adopted to new institutions and cultural forms, decrying the old ways of tribal socio-political life The new middle class elites demanded democratization of traditional political institutions which meant abolition of many of the rights and privileges of the Chiefs.

The concept of freedom coming to a people who had never known any measure of political power before had undoubtedly led to a certain amount of licence.[20] However beyond the attempt to curtail the chiefs' powers, the new leadership failed to spell out any clear political goal. Even when the eclipse of colonial power was so imminent, the best course they could visualize was to remain under colonial rule for another three to five years during which, they hoped, they would learn how to run their own government and the chiefs, ruling under some constitution, would no longer be a burden on the common people.[21]

It was at this stage that the Middle class, primarily consisting of the intelligentsia among the Hills of Manipur took a concrete Shape. L. K. Mahapatra described the role of the intelligentsia among tribals in the following terms, 'The intelligentsia are to be conceived as the interpreters of the foreign, impinging culture, with which they have already developed some familiarity, much ahead of the masses. The foreign culture in India is not merely Western civilisation in India, but the whole framework of a social order where one had to understand the ways of the courts, the bureaucracy, the political parties and of several distant groups of people for a common cause'.[22] The Numbers of Missionary schools and the State Government educational Policy in 1885 the school of the British Agent later known as Johnstone Higher secondary school, after its founder Sir James Johnstone accentuated the growth of the Middle class. During 1893-94, two L. P. Schools, one at Sekmai and another at Mao Thana were opened. In 1895, Tera Keithel L. P. School and Pettigrew L. P. School were established.[23] Gradually, after Independence the number of Hill people settling in the valleys for education grew. After the establishment of English schools in the hill and the valleys, the new group of middle class steadily increased.

Urbanisation too contributed to the rise of middle class. A remarkable consequence of The Anglo-Kuki War was the decision to constitute four subdivisions including those for the hill areas, in an open darbar held at the palace of Manipur, on 16th October 1919 by the Chief Commissioner, Sir Nicholas Beatson Bell:

1) One sub-division at Imphal.
2) One sub-division for the south west area inhabited by the Kukis with headquarters at Churachandpur.
3) One sub-division for the North West inhabited by the Kabui Naga, Kacha Nagas and Kukis with headquarters at Tamenglong.
4) One sub-division Northeast for Tangkhul Nagas and Kukis with headquarters at Ukhrul.

On 1st January 1930, a re-arrangement of the Hill administration was made and according to this, three sub-divisions were abolished and withdrawn from the hills and located at Imphal with two sub-divisions: Sub-division (north) and Sub-division (south) under the President of the Manipur State Darbar. After the execution of Jadonang (1931) and capture of Gaidinliu (1932), the Tamenglong Sub-divisions namely: Tamenglong, Ukhrul, and Sadar were created till the colonial period. The flow of Hill people to the valley gained momentum. Whoever managed to raise his position in the village migrated to the town. The creations of the following sub-divisions for administrative convenience provided access to the hill people from the interior parts of the state to modern amenities, education and medical facilities. Henceforth, the hill people were anxious to migrate to towns; the establishment of the sub-divisions gave incentives for the growth of towns in the hill areas.

It provided for a faster growth of the middle class. As a result, every village had a number of educated middle class, who began to take the initiating role bringing awareness, and narrating events that occurred within the rest of India and the outside world to the villages. These new middle class of educated people earned the respect of their respective villages and their successes were looked upon with awe. They began to take an important and decisive role in society and contributed to the growth of political consciousness especially the question of ethnic-Identity. The new middle class rallied for the formation of various Associations on religious, social and cultural lines to safeguard their interest and identity. Some of such associations were Tangkhul Katamnao Long, Kuki Innpi Manipur, The Officers Association of Nagas or Kukis etc. The middle class exercised tremendous influence in the socio-cultural, economic and political life. With the emergence of the middle class, the tribal society in Manipur was transformed into a complex society. As such, the middle class can be classified into three stratification. The Upper middle class, the middle-middle class and the lower middle class. The Meiteis had become sanskritized in the 17th century and the introduction of the caste system created new divisions in society. In the tribal society, the educated people themselves created social stratification.

A tentative classification would be as follows: During the colonial period, the upper strata comprised of the chiefs, Lambus, government officials, the early converts; while the lower class comprised of the gentry and the illiterate villagers and the middle class comprised of the educated few. Later in the post Independence period, the senior bureaucrats, Ministers, Executive members of the District Council and the higher grade of contractors formed the creamy layer. In the middle rung, the next rung was composed of teachers, professors, members of the legislative councils and state legislatures, Leaders of various church organizations, gazetted government officials, lawyers and doctors, lower grade employees, Entrepreneurs and NGO's, small scale business owners, lower grade contractors, while the lower middle class comprised of the fourth grade government employees, petty traders etc. It was in this confusing state that the intelligentsia (educated masses) began to play a dominant role in questioning the authority of the Chiefs, the monopoly of the church leaders, the role of the Ministers and thus asserted the demand for maintaining their own identity on ethnic lines.

ASSERTION OF ETHNIC IDENTITY

Ethnicity is a new concept in social science. It was first used by David Rieman in 1853 as referred to in the 1972 Supplement of the Oxford English Dictionary and subsequently by Cynthia H. Enloe and in India by J. Das Gupta.[24] The concept of ethnic group and ethnicity is rather nebulous. In modern times, an ethnic group is sometime interchangeably used for a nationality, a minority, a tribe, a community a culture, a society, a race, a people, or a nation.[25] Nationalism is primarily a political principle, which holds that the political and the national unit should be congruent.[26] Nationalism is also a method of teaching the right – determination of the will.[27] In most cases, the term ethnic community and ethnos have been used to mean "people". In such instances 'all kinds of ethnic communities-nations, nationalities, tribes, (or groups of related tribes) are included.[28] An ethnic community is a social organism consolidated on a definite territory from groups of people under the condition (already present, or achieved by them in the course of the development of economic and socio-cultural connection) of a common language, common feature of culture and a way of life, a number of common social values and traditions. The basic characteristics of an ethnic community are ethnic self-consciousness and a common name for themselves (self-naming) or (imposed from without) a common language, territory, peculiarities of psychological traits, common culture and way of life, and a definite form of social and territorial organization, or an aspiration to create such an organization.[29]

Nationalism is usually associated with a state of independence, formation of nations, particularly during 1st World War and 2nd World War. The concept of nationalism is emphasized in relation to unification under a common identity. Identity based on nationalism is stressed based on Smith's observation, 'They add to one's psychological sense of security'. Nationalism is also important because it is about "land", both in terms of possession and (literal) rebuilding, and of belonging where forefathers lived and where history demarcates a "homeland".[30] Usually ethnic groups which became a minority claim special privileges to preserve their culture, language, etc. E. Hunter and Philip speak about ethnic minority; ethnic minorities are social groups, which are distinguished from the larger society of which they form a part by certain traits, such as language, national origin, religion, race, values or customs.

The Kuki and Naga national movement is based on the ethnic concept. The British popularized the term 'Kuki' and 'Naga', giving a common identity, since the early 19th century for their colonial administration and ethnographic convenience. The British who subjugated and conquered these two tribes and brought them under their administration had directly or indirectly created a feeling of isolation and separateness' from Indians and the Myanmarese.

NAGA IDENTITY

The name 'Naga' is a generic term applied to a number of sub-tribes, who were otherwise known by different names: Ao, Angami, Lotha, Sema, Tangkhul, Mao, Maram, Zeliangrong, etc. The origin of the generic term 'Naga' is shrouded in mystery. Till today there is no definite answer to this question of the origin of the name 'Naga'. But many scholars have put forward different views as to the origin of the name 'Naga'. There are three prominent hypotheses regarding its origin, viz., (i) the '*Nanga*' meaning 'paucity of cloth' hypothesis of L. W. Shakespeare (1914), Robert Reid (1942), William Robinson (1841), Johnstone (2002) and E. W. Dun (1981); (ii) the '*Nok*' meaning 'people or folk' hypothesis of S. E. Peal (1894), E. Gait (1963) and V. Elwin (1960) and (iii) the '*Naka*' meaning 'pierced ears' hypothesis of R. R. Shimray (1985). Whatever may be the origin of the name 'Naga', it is widely accepted that the name was given by the people of Brahmaputra and Barak valleys.[31] With the consolidation of British rule and spread of Christianity, the use of the name 'Naga' has been popularized and consequently accepted by these sub-tribes.

However, in Manipur the use of the name 'Naga' among the tribes, who are now identified as 'Naga', is a post World War II phenomena. Though the British had used the name to identify and classify the tribes of Manipur, it was not very popular. It is evident when Jadonang and Gaidinliu launched the anti-British movement in 1931 they had not termed it as Naga movement rather it was 'Kabui' and 'Kutcha' Naga movement. Again, Shimray (1985: 39), in his boyhood, told the Japanese forces during the World War II that they were Tangkhuls and not Nagas when the latter addressed them as Nagas. This only indicates that the Naga identity was in flux even in the middle of the 20th century. Tangkhul, Tarao and Zeliangrong were all separate tribes with their own distinct identity.[32]

GROWTH OF NAGA NATIONALISM IN MANIPUR

Nagas are the second largest group in the state. They occupy 55 per cent (approximately in 2001 Census) of the total geographical area of the state. There are 18 Naga sub-tribes in Manipur. They are: Aimol, Anal, Chiru, Chothe, Kharam, Koireng, Kom, Maring, Mayon, Monshang, Lamkang, Mao, Maram, Thangal, Poumai, Tangkhul, Tarao and Zeliangrong.[33]

The Naga experience in 1st World War is mainly responsible for the subsequent rise of Naga nationalism, sometime in the early 20th century which also marked the beginning of The Naga National Movement.[34] The Naga relation with the British (1832-1947) produced mixed and contradictory consequences on the one hand, the Nagas were made aware of their distinctive identity (today referred to as the unique history of the Nagas) and also became conscious of their rights this lead them towards modernisation and a more holistic world view. On the other hand, the Nagas lost their sovereignty and much of significance in their culture in the process of modernization, even as they (Nagas) were divided geo-politically and placed under two nations states-India and Myanmar.[35] The growth of nationalism among the Nagas of Manipur can be traced back to the first half of the 20th century. The indirect influence of 1st World War was tremendous. The Nagas brought horrific accounts as to how the great civilized nations fought for their ends and interests while Nagas were condemned as barbarous for their head-hunting wars. Secondly, the intercourse among the different Nagas of different tribes in France far from their homes, created a sense of political unity, fostered mutual love and a sense of self-respect which manifested itself in their verbal resolution, that on return to their land they would work for friendship and unity among themselves and give up practices like head-hunting and village feuds which weakened the Nagas as a whole. It was this spirit, which spearheaded an upsurge of the Naga Nationalist movement.[36] The British rule brought many changes in the age-old traditional tribal society. They had to pay a house tax of ₹ 3 per annum; the amount though nominal was regarded as a burden as they were not required to pay any tax before the establishment of the British rule. Moreover, the spread of Christianity was a major cause of concern, though almost all the tribals in course of time became Christians, as it was a superimposition of foreign religion and practices over the traditional beliefs and practices. Jadonang and Gaidinliu rose in revolt against the British in 1930, which may be termed as a revivalist movement of the Zeliangrongs. The superimposition of the new religion, the persistence of superstitious practices of the old religion and growing disunity among these tribes were the main reasons for Jadonang and Gaidinliu to rise in revolt against the British. The movement took a semi-military, semi-religious and semi-political character.[37]

The movement, however, was finally subdued with the capture of both Jadonang and Gaidinliu. Jadonang was sentenced to death by Higgins, the then Political Agent of Manipur and the sentence was carried out on 29 August 1931 at Imphal. Gaidinlu was arrested on 17 October 1932 and was sentenced to life imprisonment but was released after Independence.

While in Nagaland, with the formation of Naga National Council (NNC), the growth of nationalism took an anti-Indian turn, the Nagas of Manipur were not integrated with the movement. The Nagas of Manipur were neither a signatory to the memorandum submitted by the Naga Club to the Simon Commission nor took part in Phizo's plebiscite of 1951 on the question of Nagas' independence. Moreover, the Nagas of Manipur were not included in the proposed idea of 'unified Nagaland' as demanded by the Naga Peoples' Convention (NPC) in 1957. The leaders of NPC only demanded for unification of the Tuensang division of North Eastern Frontier Agency and not any Naga inhabited areas of Manipur.[38] Rani Gaidinliu, one of the leading revivalist Naga social reformers and freedom fighters, after her release from jail in 1947, opposed Phizo's demand for independence. She even went underground to organize her people to fight against the NNC militants. Under her leadership Naga nationalism in Manipur, based on traditional Naga culture, emerged as an alternative force to NNC dominated Naga nationalism based on Christianity and western culture.[39] The criticism of 'Naga Raj movement' was made by Christian writers because of the conflict between Rani Gaidinliu and the underground Nagas whose declared objective was to make, 'Nagaland for Christ', and the members of the Heraka cult of Rani Gaidinliu in 1963.[40] Thus, Gaidinliu inspired nationalistic ideas of the Nagas of Manipur came in direct conflict with the NNC inspired Naga nationalism of

Nagaland. This rivalry between the two groups advocating of Naga nationalism, however, gradually died down following the surrender of Gaidinliu and her followers in 1966.[41] This conflict was however patched up by the Zeliangrong Naga Union

Although, the Naga nationalistic territorial claim over the Naga inhabited areas of Manipur was tacitly legitimized for the first time when the 1964 Indo-Naga Cease-fire was extended to Ukhrul, Mao and Tamenglong, even then some prominent leaders of the Nagas under the banner of All Tribal Delegation went to Delhi in May, 1970 to demand statehood for Manipur and stuck to the stand to remain with Manipur instead of acceding to Nagaland.[42]

However, the demand for unification of Naga inhabited areas in Manipur with Nagaland got a boost following the declaration of Indian National Congress that it did not consider the Naga integration movement as anti-party, anti-national and unconstitutional activity (www.satp.org). The demand for unification was brought into sharp focus following the establishment, and ascendance to hegemony, of the National Socialist Council of Nagaland (NSCN) and subsequently NSCN (Isak-Muivah) [NSCN (I-M)]. In fact, NSCN (I-M) has bridged the Naga aspirations for unification across Nagaland and Manipur. As the Tangkhuls have become the backbone of the Naga army under NSCN (I-M), who form the majority of the Naga population in Manipur, the voice of the Nagas may be treated as equivalent to the voice of the NSCN (I-M). The strategy of NSCN (I-M) to engage the Government of India through peace overtures and effecting the merger of Naga inhabited hills of Manipur as part of the bargain backfired on the face of stiff opposition from the Meiteis and Naga nationalism in Manipur turned assertive and restive. NSCN (I-M) mobilized the Nagas of Manipur through Naga social organizations like United Naga Council, Manipur (UNCM), All Naga Students'

Association, Manipur (ANSAM) and Naga Women's Union, Manipur (NWUM). In fact, the question of unification has put the Nagas of Manipur in a dilemma. While the Christian Nagas in general and Christian Nagas under the influence of NSCN (I-M) in particular are, explicitly or tacitly, in favor of unification, but non-Christian Nagas in general and a segment of the politically active Christian Nagas other than NSCN (I-M) are in favour of status quo.

Before sovereignty was transferred to India and Burma, the British did not make any arrangement towards the unification of the Nagas into one administrative unit. The NNC were demanding a sovereign Nagaland state comprising all Naga inhabited hills of Assam, Manipur and Burma. At the same time, the Naga leaders in Manipur were also making efforts to integrate particularly the Naga areas of Mao, Ukhrul, Tamenglong, Sadar hills, Tengnoupal and Churachandpur sub-divisions of Manipur. But they could not raise the issue of common cause of all the Naga people.[43]

Thus, the Naga nationalism in Manipur has two dimensions. Initially, it started against the British rule and the spread of Christianity under the banner of Jadonang and Gaidinlieu. However, in the later stage, especially after the dominance of NSCN (I-M), the aspirations of the Nagas of Manipur have merged with the goal of unification of Nagas as professed by NSCN (I-M). This aspiration of the Nagas has led to anti-Meitei feeling and Meiteis are seen as an obstacle to their goal for Naga unification. Although a segment of the Nagas does not favour any realignment of the territorial boundary of Manipur, they are, however, in a minority. Besides the Meiteis and Nagas, Kukis are the third largest group in Manipur. As the Nagas and Kukis have overlapping settlements in many parts of Manipur hills, the Naga movement for unification has a direct bearing upon the livelihood and security of the Kukis. This has led to the politicization of the Kuki community and the emergence of Kuki nationalism.

KUKI IDENTITY

The Kukis were first heard of in 1777 during the Governor Generalship of Warren Hastings, when these tribes frequently attacked the British subjects in Chittagong.[44] They were, however, heard of in Manipur in between 1830 and 1840. In 1845, their large scale migration caused anxiety to the old Kuki inhabitants of the hill people.[45] In order to bring a solution to the problem, Mc Culloch, the then Political Agent of Manipur, allotted land and settled them down in such a manner that they acted as guards on exposed frontiers. Following Mc Culloch's policy, in 1855 the British Government settled a large colony of Kukis to the east of North Cachar and beyond the Langting River to act as a barrier against the Naga raids in North Cachar.[46]

Like the term Naga, the Kuki is also a generic term applied to the various sub-tribes, viz., Thadou, Paite, Hmar, Simte, Zou, Gangte, Vaiphei, Guite, Ralte, Sukte, etc. In Manipur, they were known as 'Khongjais' before the use of the term Kuki. However, it is still not known for certain as to the origin of the generic term 'Kuki'. There are three views regarding the origin of the term Kuki: (i) it is derived from a word applied to a system of cultivation by the Bengalis,[47] (ii) it is derived from the Baluchisthan word '*Kuchis*' meaning 'wandering people', and (iii) it is derived from the English word '*Kooky*' meaning 'peculiar or unusual people'.[48] Though no definite answer is found as to the origin of the term Kuki, it is widely accepted that it was given by outsiders.

GROWTH OF KUKI NATIONALISM IN MANIPUR

The growth of Kuki nationalism also started, like the Nagas, initially through mobilization of the Kukis against the British. Kuki nationalism was first manifested against colonialist' inquest into Kuki territory in the eighteenth century.[49] The anti-British position of the Kukis in Manipur hills can be traced to at least three reasons. Firstly, the administration of hill areas of Manipur was directly entrusted to the Vice-president of the State Durbar, who was a British subject. He was assisted by Manipuri *lambus* in the affairs of the administration, who were mere peons and interpreters, but exercised much authority during the British rule. This hurt the sentiments of the Kuki chiefs who considered themselves at par with the Maharaja of Manipur. Such an administrative set up created a gap between the people and the officials. Secondly, the economic condition of the Kukis worsened with the imposition of house tax of ₹ 3 per annum and the obligation of free labour under the system of *pothang*, which they disliked. Thirdly, the conditions of the Kukis were further worsened when they were sent to France as Labour Corps during the 1st World War, much against their will. Then the blow came when the government gave a second calling for such recruitment. This time the Kuki chiefs did not give in easily to the British and they resisted all forms of British action towards recruitment.[50] This incident which is popularly known as 'Kuki Rebellion' in imperial historiography might be seen as the anti-colonial freedom struggle of the Kukis. This anti-colonial struggle had cemented the relationship of the Kukis across the villages and brought the Chiefs closer to each other. The Kuki identity was also strengthened.

In the wake of World War II Kukis joined the Indian National Army, and together with the imperial Army of Japan fought the British again. There are about 150 Kuki INA pensioners, 80 of these listed in the Freedom Fighters of Manipur.[51] Defeat of the Axis powers dashed the hopes of the Kukis to be restored to their pre-British state of freedom. With the British raj ending, the Kukis formed the Kuki National Assembly (KNA), in October 1946, to press forward the cause of the Kukis and demand for a homeland for themselves. With the merger of Manipur into the Indian Union in 1949, this demand subsided. However, with the Nagas and other tribal groups in the region getting their homelands, the young generations of the Kukis became restive. Creation of Nagaland in 1963 and Mizoram statehood in 1973 provided an incentive to the Kukis. Following World War II, the Kukis were tense and wary and began to deliberate on the political future of the Kukis. The KNA also planned to establish a pan-Kuki platform for the Kukis in Manipur. Hence, in 1947 a Kuki-Naga Unity Committee was formed but with little success (Resolution no. 1, 27, May 1947, of the Kuki Naga Unity Conference held at Mao Naga Village. Mr. Lunneh (Kuki) presided over the conference, and Mr. Lorho (Naga) as the secretary. Finally the KNA became "a symbol of Kuki opposition to the Nagas". In 1947, the KNA formally opposed the Naga claim to the land of the Kukis.[52] The sense of urgency-increased manifold with the NSCN gaining ground in the hills of Manipur from 1980 and the Naga demand for unification becoming vociferous. With the ascendancy of the NSCN (I-M) in the driver's seat since 1988, Kukis have recognized that Naga aspirations pose serious threat to their livelihood. The realization that without a well-demarcated homeland the future of the Kukis is insecure has penetrated deep into the psyche of the Kuki community. The failure of KNA to address the livelihood threats faced by the community has led to the birth of a plethora of Kuki underground organizations leading to the transformation of the Kuki movement for homeland into a militant movement.

The demand for a Kuki homeland called 'Zale'n-gam': land of freedom' was spearheaded with the formation of an underground government called Kuki National Organisation (KNO) and its armed wing Kuki National Army (KNA) in 1988 under the leadership of Pu Thangkholun, a Manipuri Kuki. The main objective of KNO is to carve out a homeland for the Kukis, i.e., 'Kukiland', one in India and the other in Myanmar.[53] Similarly, Nehlun Kipgen, a Manipuri Kuki, formed the Kuki National Front (KNF) in 1988 with the objective of carving out an autonomous 'Kukiland' under the Constitution of India.[54] However, the territorial claims of the Kukis overlap the territorial claims of the Nagas in Manipur. This overlapping territorial interest has brought the two communities into a conflicting situation. The Nagas see the Kukis as a barrier on the way to their long cherished goal for unification. The territorial claims of the Kukis include the districts of Churachandpur, Chandel and some portions of Tamenglong, Senapati and Ukhrul, whereas the Nagas claim the districts of Tamenglong, Senapati, Ukhrul and Chandel. Thus, the Kukis and Nagas have overlapping and conflicting territorial interests over all the hill districts of Manipur, except Churachandpur. In the midst of these conflicting claims, a rival Party called Khulmi National Union was formed of various clans, excepting those associated with Thadou. In July 1947, at the Thanlon Area Chiefs Conference, votes were cast to choose a national identity from amongst Khul, Kuki and Mizo. However, the success of Khulmi National Union was short lived.[55]

Further splinter groups from Kuki National Assembly emerged: the Hmar Congress (1954) and the Hmar national Union (1962), the Paite National Council (1956), the Gangte Tribal Union (1958) (Chaube, Hill politics in North East India, 1973. Added to this, is the Thadou-Kuki imbroglio.

This conflicting territorial claim (Nagas-Kukis) has turned into inter-tribal warfare in 1990's because the Nagas at the behest of NSCN (I-M) asserted their supremacy over the Kukis[57] (For details of the Naga-Kuki conflict, Singh, 2008). One important implication of the conflict is the proliferation of Kuki underground organizations. The failure of the state to protect the Kukis from the onslaught of the Nagas, especially NSCN (I-M), during the conflict, gave birth to Kuki Liberation Army (KLA), Kuki Revolutionary Army (KRA), Zomi Revolutionary Organisation (ZRO) and United Kuki Liberation Front (UKLF). The failure of the KNA and KNF to meet to the expectations of the people to protect their interests and to resist the onslaught of the NSCN (I-M) has sent strong signals to every Kuki sub-tribe to create their own self-defence mechanism. The multiplicity of Kuki militant organizations may be seen as the resultant reaction of this social insecurity that has arisen out of the Naga-Kuki conflict of 1990s.

Another implication is the large scale displacement of the Kukis from conflict-ridden areas and their subsequent settlement in Churachandpur district, the safe homeland of the Kukis, which has destabilized the host society. The large scale migration of the Thadous had created some unrest among the other sub-tribes of Kukis like Paite, Simte, Zou, Vaiphei, etc. for fear of being outnumbered. Intra-Kuki antagonism arising out of the dominating attitude of the Thadous is believed to be the prime factor behind the onset of Kuki-Paite clash in 1997 [For details of Kuki-Paite clash,[58] and the consequent formation of Zomi Revolutionary Army (ZRA), the armed wing of ZRO, to protect the other Kuki sub-tribes from the dominance of Thadous all?

Thus, the Kuki identity, developed during the colonial rule in the north eastern hills of British India, was consolidated through anti-British rebellion during 1917-19. However, the

Naga-Kuki conflict has led to the further consolidation of the Kuki identity. The political mobilization of the members of the Kuki community in support of a 'Kuki homeland' has transformed itself into a nationality. The Kuki nationalism is, thus, an outcome of the search of the Kukis for a homeland of their own. In fact, the demands for 'Kuki homeland' and 'unification of Nagas' are mutually exclusive. This has given rise to a serious inter-tribal animosity between Nagas and Kukis. The national sentiments of the Kukis were also severely hurt as the state of Manipur utterly failed to protect the lives of the innocent Kukis in the wake of the Naga-Kuki conflict (1990's). The Kuki nationalism, thus, stands aloof in an amazingly complex ethno-political matrix in Manipur in search of a homeland of their own.

Among the Kukis, conflicting issues sprang up over the Nomenclature, "Kuki"; while some adhere to Kuki, despite its deletion from the recognized tribes of Manipur, for a common identity of all Kuki tribes, others propounded terminology such as 'Chin', 'Mizo' 'Zo' 'Khulmi'. The Pan-Kuki movement seems to be moving nowhere. Much of the tribal identity crisis took a new dimension when the scheduled Castes and scheduled tribes Lists was modified and announced in 1956, that list contained only 29 tribal groups, in Manipur. The Kukis who were earlier recognized were deleted from the list of 1956 and took it as the most grave injustice done upon their community.[59] In 2003 'Any Kuki tribes' was introduced. Signs of reversal from a state of near disintegration to reunification of the Kukis have started since then. After Independence, the period from 1940 is a period of flux due to perplexing innumerable internal issues of the Kukis. However, the reintroduction of any Kuki tribes in 2003 in Manipur, and Suspension of Operations signed in 2008 among Government of India and, KNO and the State government of Manipur has changed the status-quo. A semblance of loose pan-Kuki unity has crystallised among the various Kuki ethnic groups.

Within the Nagas too, internal squabbles in the Naga leadership had greatly weakened the Naga movement. Due to Indian military pressure, the underground Nags signed an accord with the government of India, represented by the governor of Nagaland at Shillong. The Shillong Accord created further furore among the Nagas, both the supporters and opponents. It was condemned by the FGN ranks as well as leaders and led to the split in the Naga movement. The younger leadership consisting of Isak Swu who was relieved of his post in1988, Thiungaleng Muivah, General Secretary of the NNC, a follower of late R. Suisa and an eastern Naga leader, S. S. Khaplang, formed a new outfit known as the Nationalist Socialist Council of Nagaland (NSCN).[60] It split into two factions the NSCN (IM) and the NSCN (K). The former is led by chairman Isak Swu and Th. Muivah, while the latter by its vice-president S. S. Khaplang. The NSCN (IM) which had more cadres in Manipur State attacked the NNC and FGN cadres. The NSCN (IM) concluded a ceasefire Agreement with Government of India in 1997. Starting from1st August1997, it continued for more than five years and several rounds of talks had been held with the Government of India since then. This is an ongoing process.

CONCLUSION

The new consciousness that led to the emergence of a new middle class forged a common identity amongst its members. On the other hand conversions to Christianity, introduction of modern education and advancement in literacy has resulted in the growth of a new political awareness that has lead to the assertion of ethnic identity. Recognition of Manipur's tribals in the Scheduled Castes and Schedule tribes list offers some benefits, but also created room for further inter-rivalries and apprehensions, insecurities as all tribals did not benefit evenly from its benefits. In fact, it was the middle class which apportioned for itself the benefits arising from being classed as Scheduled Tribes whereas those living in remote hill hamlets lost out. Nonetheless, tension and strife resulting from assertion of identity was partly due to the apathy and lack of understanding by the Government of India. (In common parlance, Manipur is regarded as being on the periphery in contrast to 'mainland India') A combination of external and internal factors has escalated the Kuki-Naga identity movement. In the colonial period, most of the tribes were not conscious of their ethno-tribal identities and their world was confined to their family, clan, and village. The term Naga-Kuki was given as part of the colonial 'divide and rule' policy. In the post–Independence era crystallization of a nation base on ethnic identity emerged.

REFERENCE

1. Fernandes, Leela, *India's New Middle Class: Democratic Politics in an Era of Economic Reform*. University of Minnesota Press, 2006. p. 53.
2. Ray, B. Datta, *The Emergence and Role of Middle Class in North East India*, Uppal Publishing House, 1983. p. 14.
4. Gangte, T. S., *The Kukis of Manipur*, Gyan Publishing, New Delhi, Second Edition, 2003. p. 5.
4. Allen, B. C., *Gazetteer of Naga Hills and Manipur*, Mittal Publication, 1905, p. 60.
5. Brown, R., *Statistical Account of Manipur*, Mittal Publication, New Delhi, 2001. p. 25.

6. Mackenzie, A., *The North East Frontier of Bengal*, Mittal Publication, New Delhi, Reproduced, 2005. p. 86.
7. Gangte, T. S., *The Kukis, op. cit.* p. 124.
8. Carey, Bertram S. & Tuck, H. N., *The Chin Hills Vol. I & II*, Firma KLM Calcutta, 1976. Reprinted. p. 10.
9. Brown, R., *op. cit.* p. 19.
10. Wallerstein, Immanuel, *Social Change, The Colonial Situation*, John Wiley and Sons, INC, New York, 1966. pp. 3-5.
11. *Ibid.* p. 5.
12. Dena, Lal, *History of Modern Manipur: 1826-1946*, Orbit Publishers, New Delhi, 1991. pp. 80-81.
13. Joykumar, N., *Social Movements in Manipur*, Mittal Publication, New Delhi, 2005. pp. 46-47.
14. Kabui, Gangmumei, *The History of the Zeliangrong Nagas – From Makhel to Rani Gaidinliu*, Spectrum Publications, Guwahati, 2004. pp. 128-129.
15. Dena, Lal, *Christian Missions and Colonialism*,Vendrame Institute Shillong, 1988. p. 111.
16. Kabui, Gangmumei, *op. cit.* p. 141.
17. Dena, Lal, *op. cit.* p. 40.
18. Kabui, Gangmumei, *op. cit.* p. 132.
19. Haokip, Seilen, *Rhetorics of Kuki Nationalism*, Lustra Print, New Delhi, 2010. p. 30.
20. Report of Rev. Basil E Jones submitted to the Mission Committee at Liverpool as a basis for discussion on the future educational policy to be pursued in Lushai hills (1924-1947), in Lal Dena, *Christian Missions an Colonialism*,1988. p. 7.
21. Lalremchuani Sena, 'The Mizo Independence Movement', Unpublished M.A. Dissertation submitted to the Californian State University, 1974, p. 31.
22. Downs, Frederick, *Social Movements Among Tribes of India. Essays on Christianity in North East India*, Delhi, 1983. p. 181.

23. Devi, Jamini, *Education in Manipur*, 1989, *op. cit.* p. 46.
24. Ray, B. Datta, *Tribal Identity and Tension in North East India*, Omsons Publications, 1989. p. 1.
25. Lewis, C.S. cit. in R. Vashum, *Nagas Right for Self Determination*, Mittal Publications, New Delhi, 2000. pp. 45-46.
26. Gellner, Ernest Andre, *Nations and Nationalism: New Perspectives on the Past Series*, Publisher Ithaca, NY Cornell University Press, 1988. p. 1.
27. Kedourie, Elie, *Nationalism*, Publisher, Wiley-Blackwell, Fourth Expanded Edition, 1993. p. 76.
28. Bromley, David B., & Dennis Basil Bromley, *The Psychology of Human Aging*, Penguin group, New Zealand, Revised, 1974. p. 56.
29. Kozlov, M. A., 'Paleobiology Database', *Paleontological Journal* 7, 1974. p. 86.
30. Smith, Anthony A., *National Identity*, Penguin, London, 1991, pp. 72-74.
31. Kabui, 1995. *op. cit.* p. 24.
32. Singh, A. *Koireng, Ethnicity and Inter-Community Conflicts: A case of Kuki-Naga in Manipur*, Akansha Publishing House, New Delhi, 2008. p. 53.
33. *Ibid.*
34. Vashum, R., Nagas: *Right to Self Determination*, Mittal Publication, New Delhi, 2000. p. 57.
35. Vashum, R., *ibid.* pp. 60-61
36. Horam, *The Rising Nagas*, pp. 125-126.
37. Singh, N. Joykumar, *Social Movements in Manipur*, Mittal Publications, New Delhi, 1992. *op. cit.* pp. 56-67.
38. Nag, Sajal, "Naga Identity: Formation, Construction and Expansion," in C. J. Thomas and Gurudas Das (Ed.), *Dimensions of Development in Nagaland*, Regency Publications, New Delhi, 2002. p. 150.

39. Stracey, P. D., *Nagaland Nightmare*, Allied Publishers, New Delhi, 1968. p. 44.
40. Kabui, Gangmumei, *The History of Zeliangrong Nagas*, p. 291.
41. Singh, Prakash, *Nagaland*, National Book Trust, New Delhi, 1995 (4th ed.). *op. cit.* p. 26.
42. *Ibid. op. cit.* p. 50
43. Horam, *The Rising Nagas*, *op. cit.* pp. 369-372.
44. Gangte, T. S., *The Kukis of Manipur: A Historical Analysis*, Gyan Publishing House, New Delhi, 1993. Op. cit. p. 19.
45. Johnstone, James, *Manipur and the Naga Hills*, Gyan Publishing House, New Delhi, 2002. p. 45.
46. Ray, Asok Kumar, *Authority and Legitimacy: A Study of the Thadou-Kukis in Manipur*, Renaissance Publishing House, Delhi, 1990. p. 28.
47. Dun, E.W., *Gazzetteer of Manipur*, Vivek Publishing Company, New Delhi, 1981 (reprint). p. 32.
48. Vaiphei, S. Prim, The Kukis in Sanajaoba, in (Ed.), *Manipur Past and Present*, vol. 3, Mittal publication, New Delhi, 1995. op. cit. p. 126.
49. Haokip, Sielen, *Rhetorics of Kuki Nationalism, A Treatise*, Lustra print, New Delhi, 2010. p. 15.
50. Singh, N. Joykumar, *Social Movements in Manipur*, 1992. *op. cit.* pp. 43-55.
51. *Freedom Fighters of Manipur*, published in 1985, Congress Centenary year, by freedom fighters cell, MPCC in Dr. Seilen, *Rhetorics of Kuki Nationlism*. p. 24.
52. Haokip, Seilen, ibid, Resolution No. 1 KNA meeting concerning the Aimol and Tamenglong Circles held at Bolkot village, dated 8 June1947. p. 26.
53. Haokip, P. S., *Zale'n-gam: The Kuki Nation*, Kuki National Organisation, Zale'n-gam 2008 (Rev. ed.). pp. 376-377, 403
54. Kipgen, Donn Morgan, 2006, *The Great Betrayal: Brief Notes on Kuki Insurgency Movement.* http://manipuronline.com

55. Vaiphei, S. Prim. *op. cit.* p. 128.
56. Chaube, Shibani Kinkar, *Hill Politics in Northeast India*, Orient Longman, Calcutta, 1999. p. 195.
57. Singh, A. Koireng, *op. cit.*
58. Singh, S. Mangi, 'The Kuki-Paite Clash (1997-98) in Manipur', in N. Joykumar Singh (ed.), *Ethnic Relations Among the People of North-East India*, Centre for Manipur Studies, Manipur University and Akansha Publishing House, New Delhi, 2006. pp. 61-73.
59. Ray, R. Datta., *Tribal Identity and Tension in North East India*, p. 38.
60. Kabui, Gangmumei, *History of the Zeliangrong Nagas*, pp. 221-222.

Five

The Effects of Globalisation

Globalisation is a multifaceted term with many possible interpretations that fall into the categories of economics, polity, society, environment, culture and even food habits. Globalisation refers specially to the movement from isolated economies to a global economy. Thus, Globalisation could best be defined as the increasing "interconnectedness of the world through new systems of communication",[1] affecting all areas of life. Globalisation initially went hand in hand with liberalization and pertained initially to the field of economies especially import and export of goods and services. In the light of such a wide connotation and broad application, it becomes necessary to study its impact among the tribals of Manipur in different spheres, and how it hastens the process of modernisation in their society.

As such, indigenous people are on the cusp of crisis in sustainable development. The impact of globalization is strongest on these populations. Their communities are concrete examples of sustainable societies, historically evolved in diverse ecosystems. Today, they face the challenges of survival and renewal in a globalised world. The indigenous people are unaware of these great transitionary changes and therefore they are easily swept aside by invincible hands of the markets and its proponents.

Globalization is not merely a question of marginalization for indigenous peoples, it is a multipronged attack on the very foundation of their existence and livelihoods. This ever-increasing capacity to communicate worldwide has resulted in the increasing domination of western cultures, whose economics, and political institutions are most affluent and powerful. This process has had profound effects on less powerful cultures. Today development planners in the name of so-called development work are gradually and increasingly eroding ethnic diversity, challenging the homogenizing tendency of economists to reduce populations to quantifiable groups.

As Rangarajan, contended globalisation is more than just about economics. It is not only about the ratio of exports to Gross Domestic Product (GDP) but also about culture, society, politics and people.[2] Henceforth, globalisation becomes a problem from the cultural identity perspective too. In the global economy, culture has almost become a one-way operating manner of imposing the culture by rich and affluent powerful countries. It invaded the world's markets, placing people and cultures in other countries, which are unable to compete, at a disadvantage. These countries as such have difficulties in presenting the indigenous goods and services, which they produced for the world market and therefore are unable to compete with the advanced technologies. The natural result is the slow death of the self-sufficient economies of such countries, who are unable to enter the areas of influence introduced by the emerging multinational companies of developed nations.

The most disturbing element in the process of Globalisation is its relentless drive towards cultural universalism of American/European culture and associated ideological frameworks, and its implied disregard and disrespect for cultural and language diversity. There are some 350 million indigenous people in more than 70 countries around the globe, speaking autochthonous languages, and who are marginalized and frequently denied basic human rights, including their cultural rights.

Globalisation has created the world as one country, flattening the boundaries that are being erected, such as the fall of the 'Berlin Wall' and the opening of India's economy to liberalization and privatization. Trade controls were abolished in 1991, in India as Manmohan Singh, the Finance Minister at that time, and now the Prime Minister, decided that India had to open its economy. In its political aspect it has a wide ranging impact such as the latest of such events being the liberation of South Sudan, (6th July 2011) leading to democratization and identity politics in third world countries. Political and cultural identities have become part and parcel of the driving forces of democratization.

Third world societies like South Africa, Nigeria and India too have discovered that identity and cultural dynamics are intrinsic forces. While global trends in economics and politics are converging, cultural, religious and social differences seem to be widening. Globalisation and the revolution in communications technology bring people together, at the same time cause fears about loss of cultural identity. Simultaneously, literature, film, theatre, art, and dance productions often create a sense of belonging to a specific national, regional or ethnic zone. The Eighteenth century was 'the great age of happiness (but) also a time of great dissatisfaction. People had great expectation that they could have more control over their life, more religious freedom, less injustice' as stated by Florida state university Historian McMohan, the author of *Happiness: A History.*[3] Ironically it is a period where people's heightened expectations against the gap between their ideal life and their reality emerged. So also in North Eastern India, the spark had already been kindled against the colonization and emerging trend of Globalisation. Accusations of cultural imposition and domination have widely been opined in the wake of the colonial hegemony. English language emerged as a predominant position of being the lingua franca within and between global organizations and institutions. It has become the transmission belt for imposition of western goods, ideas, education and services. It also involves extensive migrations of people both within and across states, shaping a cultural fusion.

GLOBALISATION AND TRIBALS IN INDIA

India is a land with many cultures, faiths, and ways of life, dress, food habits, traditions and rituals, united like petals of one flower. Its political, economic and socio-cultural contexts occur under conditions of a multi-structural whole. The national movement and the exposure to the western culture mediated by the colonial rule made Indians very self-conscious of their cultural identity. The anxieties about the impact of Globalisation and marketisation of economy, media and information systems, the leisure and style of life etc, have today generated anxious debate among the scholars, the people and political parties. Such policy has long been in the making, but today the process of Globalisation and its impact on culture, both local and national, give it a new urgency (Singh, 1994). The word 'tribe' is generally used for a socially cohesive unit, associated with a territory, the members of which regard them as politically autonomous. Different tribes have their own cultures-dialects, life styles, social structures, rituals, values, etc., differing somewhat from those LSCAC 2010 Proceedings 152 of the dominant non-tribal peasant social groups. The forest occupies a central position in tribal culture and economy. The tribal way of life is very much dictated by the forest right from birth to death. It is ironical that the poorest people of India are living in the areas of richest natural resources. Historically, tribals have been pushed into corners owing to economic interests of various dominant groups. Colonisers have always considered tribal and indigenous people as a rare species to be studied and isolated. As such, many colonial Anthropologists of the colonial era regarded them as a subject of interest. The colonial rulers except the Christian missionaries never deemed it as part of their rule to introduce development among the tribals. Their main motive was to exploit the rich natural resources of the tribal inhabited areas. Paradoxically when individuals and groups did not meet the radicalized standard of the colonial rulers, their political and cultural rights were questioned and sometimes violated.

Recently, international indigenous organizing activities increasingly rely on similar beliefs about there being a global indigenous race that is monolithically in opposition to technology and globalization. A rise in respect for the indigenous political authority and distinct cultural practices is slowly emerging. This realization of tribal and indigenous peoples inhibits the process of decolonization and political self-determination.

From the first stirrings of capitalism, people have imagined the possibility of the world as a perfect market-unimpeded by protectionist pressures, disparate legal systems, cultural and linguistic differences, or ideological disagreement. Nevertheless, this vision has always bumped up against the world as it is actually full of sources of friction and inefficiency. Some obstacles to a frictionless global market are truly sources of waste and lost opportunities. However, some of these inefficiencies are institutions, habits, cultures and traditions that people cherish precisely because they reflect nonmarket values like social cohesion, religious faith, and national pride.[4]

Hence, the impact of Globalisation on local culture and the changing role of the nation-state can be examined by observing the particularities of the social and cultural patterns and their local, national and transnational manifestations in India. These social and cultural realities have plural character in terms of language, geography, ethnicity, religion and culture. With partial exception of the tribal population, the caste system and its related kinship structures have shaped the profile of the culture, economy and power structures within the local communities and regions. The new institutional innovations that Globalisation brings about in society are open- market, free trade and finance, communication and media, technology and science, migration and inter-cultural transactions. In social structural terms, Globalisation is a historical process of transition from the agrarian-industrial, post-industrial and finally the stage of the information society.[5]

North-East India has also experienced its share of modernization and globalization. The later part of the 19th century saw the influx of the western missionaries into the hilly regions of northeast India, and to Manipur, which still then was secluded from the rest of the country, bringing it closer to mainland India and henceforth to a global contact. The Europeans have always looked down upon the traditional culture, ideals, belief and values of the native tribes and by virtue of the 'white man's burden' they set about the task of 'civilizing' these 'uncivilized savage head hunters'. (They cut off their enemies' heads as trophies in times of war). The impact of this western enlightenment, for all that it was worth, has strongly been entrenched into the people's psyche, and it has till date, been a cause for much debate, the positive and the negative impacts always juxtaposed. Traditional culture of the people had to undergo a complete change and the educated Christian tribal had to change his or her dress code, food, religious beliefs, etc. and in the process, he or she had shed everything that defines his/her as a Kuki, Mizo, as a Naga or any of the other tribes. Those values that were once held so dear by the ancestors were constantly challenged, as they stood at odds against the new western values brought in by the missionaries. When this aspect is taken in conjunction with the study of the effects of globalization on the tribal cultures of Manipur, a number of interesting issues come to the fore.

ADVANTAGES OF GLOBALISATION

Migration from Rural to Urban Areas

One of the most visible positive effects of globalization is the migration of the hill people, who initially in the beginning flocked to the valley for education purposes. Gradually as they gained access to education, some of the few early-educated tribals found employment in the early fifties and sixties of the last century. Thereafter, many others followed and took shelter/temporary residence in the house of such educated employed tribals. These educated tribals imitated the lifestyle of the colonial officials, introducing better and improved quality of life and its attendant conveniences. The settling down of the tribals in the valley brought them into closer contact with new innovative ideas, enhances life styled, healthier food habits attitude and awareness of global knowledge and their developed a keen sense of competition. (To mention a few of the imminent tribals educated persons, mention may be made of Major B. Kathing Indian Ambassador to Myanmar; T. C. Tiankham, I.A.S.; K. Kipgen, I.A.S. among the Kuki-Chin group.) Through them, the tribals were made aware and sensitized to the new global world-view. Migrations enable them to identify their identity as a distinct indigenous group. A sense of political and national awareness enabled a tribal to rise to the position of chief minister of Manipur, Yangmasho Shaiza and Rishang Keishing succeeded as tribals to hold the seat of power as leader of the state. Thus slowly and steadily the tribals of the hills settled down in the valley forming distinct localities and communities. Many tribal inhabited areas in the valley paved the way to the establishment of Nagaram, Tangkhul Avenue, Deulahlane, Old Lambulane, New Lambulane colonies peopled by tribals.

Soon the tribals ventured further to greener pastures of urban Metros in India, for purposes of a better education, up gradation of skills, lucrative careers especially in MNC's which sprang up as a result of globalization. This migration brought them into contact with different cultures, language, usages, ideas and attitude of life, which in turn made them global citizens who through the touch of a button (Net) were able to transmit their ideas across the world and also receive new information, knowledge and ideas.

Commercialisation of Agriculture

The tribal economy was a self-sustaining economy producing for their own consumption. Basically before the advent of the British in Manipur, the agriculture produce of the country consisted principally of rice, which formed the staple article of food and the fertility of soil is so great that the crops generally prove most abundant; as stated by Captain Pemberton. Tobacco, sugar cane, indigo, mustard, the different varieties of Dal and opium are also cultivated. However, the British colonial ruler introduced new crops such as peas, potatoes, different varieties of greens and cabbages, carrots, radishes, beetroots and turnips who have been resident in the country since the late war.[6] Fruits such as oranges, Lime, pomegranate, guavas, mangoes and Jack fruits although found abundant in the valley were not commercialised. However, the British administrative policies, which introduced the imposition of Hill house tax and payment in terms of cash, forced the tribals to start selling their agricultural produce in the markets on a large scale. Thus, barter system became obsolete and cash payment took precedence. Although initially the tribals sold their agricultural produce in the market, it was only on a small scale. But after the 1940s and 1950s the commercialisation of agricultural produce boomed.

Standardised Consumer Goods

Another benefit of globalisation is in the satisfaction of customer service and the 'customer is the king' approach to production has led to improved quality of products and services. As the domestic companies have to fight foreign competition, they are compelled to raise their standards to meet the demand of customer's satisfaction in order to survive in the market. Besides, when a global brand enters a new country, it comes in riding on some goodwill, which it has to live up to. This creates competition in the market and a 'survival of the fittest' situation. With globalisation, companies have forayed into the developing countries and hence generated employment for them. It has given an opportunity to invest in the emerging markets and tap the talent, which is available there. In developing countries, there is often a lack of capital which hinders the growth of domestic companies and hence, employment. In such cases, due to global nature of the businesses, people of developing countries too can obtain gainful employment opportunities.

Development of Handloom and Handicrafts Industry

Tribal economy was based mainly on community and renewable resources. They produced for their own needs only. With the advent of globalisation revolutionary changes were effected in what were essentially cottage industries such as weaving, pottery and carpentry. The art of weaving practiced by every family to fulfill needs of clothing of family members was replaced by production for the market. A sea change occurred in terms of quality of design, colours, materials, implementing tools, infrastructure. Women puonve's (wrap around cloth) shawls of both men and women alike, basket weaving, tools and implements such as knife, daos, kitchen accessories made of woods, dry gourd of different shapes and sizes, winnowing sieve, etc were adjusted to meet the tastes of discerning consumers who demanded quality products, adjusted to global tastes. Today, if one visits the tribal markets it would be surprising to note that these handlooms and handicrafts of different hues, colours designs shape and sizes are being reproduced artistically to attract the consumers. The Lamka market or the Ukhrul market is a sight of globalisation, where modern accessories jostle with indigenous handloom materials for sale.

Impact of Media and New Technology

With the advancement in the fields of media and technology relating to different disciplines the simple tribal folks too, begin acquiring knowledge of both. There can be no doubt that new-advanced technologies in the field of pure science, medicine, nano-technology, I.T. etc. have considerably raised the quality of life of people not only in the developed but also in the developing world. The print media, through its spread of rationalism, dissemination of knowledge, path-breaking innovations has spread ideas that demythologized concepts that have been held sacred for generations. It has compelled renaissance, revival and caused revolutions in the society. It has freed people from the clutches of ignorance and superstitious practices.[7] Manipur is a state in the North East India which being seriously under-developed, has yet benefitted from the impact of globalization, particularly in the I.T. sector, which despite the absence of proper road and adequate power, has yet established links between the tribals and rest of the world. So also in the discipline of medicine and healthcare, Video-conferencing and medical transcription, the tribals have been enabled, albeit to a limited extent, to receive treatment and care for their various ailments and diseases, resulting in a decrease in infant mortality and better standard of living and longevity of life. A measure of uniformity and standardisation has become evident in monetary, commercial, land transactions etc and it is also a common sight to see tribals with Credit-cum Debit cards utilising the ATM's particularly in urban areas. They have moved a long way from the barter form of economy. In the I.T. sector, tribals are designing their own web pages, are extremely active on Face book, advertising their products, purchasing goods and tickets online, making payment online, sending and receiving Emails and exploring the possibilities of the Net. The resultant information has revolutionised their lives in more ways than one. Software becomes something you rent instead of something you own. Somebody else takes care of the upgrading and maintenance.[8] In the light of such developments, the tribals too depend on the web and tribals journals, websites, newspapers, and digital movies are increasingly produced using this technology.

Awareness of Human Rights

With awareness of world events and happenings came an awareness of constitutional rights especially those pertaining to free speech, human rights etc. In the past the tribals were governed by customary law. But Manipur having merged with India, the tribals learnt of legal rights and responsibilities and have started filing FIR's, petitions etc. especially with reference to human rights violations. The Nagas represented by Muivah have repeatedly sought Intervention to achieve their goals of sovereignty autonomy. In the deteriorating conditions of law and order, where the elite (politicians, bureaucrats, and police) are a law unto themselves, this awareness of human rights is a necessity to curb and eradicate violence and ensure peaceful conditions to pursue development and progress. By contact with other states and countries under the pervading influence of globalisation they have learnt of the struggles of other people and nations to defend their constitutional rights.

DISADVANTAGE OF GLOBALISATION

Erosion of Community-Based Economy

Globalisation has made tribals citizens of a new world order where boundaries no longer exist. In the last two decades especially, the tribals have been emulating the lifestyle of global citizens, in their manner of dress, speech, etiquette, food habits, vacations, recreational sports or hobbies, purchase of property outside Manipur, etc.

There is also sizeable tribal diaspora spread across the globe earning substantial monies, some of which makes its way back home, to raise the standard of living of their families in Manipur.

The traditional based economy of the tribals slowly eroded in the name of modernisation and globalisation. Skill and resourcefulness needed for community- living and sharing is dying out e.g. The 'Feast of Merit', which ensured that the affluent shared their riches with the common folks. Individualism emerged as the new trend. The tribals started competing among themselves for control over scarce livelihood resources, which lead to feuding, jealousy, promotion of self-interest, which in their perception were being depleted by outsiders. A Sense of Community based economy based on division of labour, (Lawm), togetherness, became extinct: the reactive of the tribals helping each other in the agricultural fields no longer exists. Rather paid individual services have become the norm, and in this process of transition to commercialized agriculture, the rich grow richer and the poor grow poorer, creating divisions in a former egalitarian society.

Erosion of Ethnic Culture

Today various cultural entities confront the dangers of globalisation. Globalisation tries to create monoculture utility services. "It is defined as a tendency to obliterate geographically based culture differences to form a worldwide culture and society. The hybridization of culture is a part of the process of globalization." It has nourished consumerism, capitalism loss of traditional values, and has resulted in the breakdown of traditional institutions like the family and community, especially of the tribal and indigenous people.[9]

The adoption of western fashions especially wedding gowns, suits, bridal bouquets, veils, cake etc, plus introduction of beauty pageants with models dressed in skimpily- clad attire is a direct fallout of globalisation. This latter trend has been adopted by the different ethnic groups living in Manipur although there is nothing repulsive in beauty pageants per se, they are highly commercialized under global influences and the prize money won by the beauty queen is more than what the average industrious hill farmer/weaver makes in a year. Capital which is needed, by artisans and weavers engaged in traditional mekhalas (puanteen/wrap around), shawls, making bead necklaces etc., is diverted to MNCs whose products are attractively packaged and displayed and which cost less than handmade products, taking cognizance of the time and labor involved in the process. Moreover being produced in conditions of individual entrepreneurship with simple and primitive tools, they lack the element of standardization. It is inevitable that MNC's earn a quick profit, their returns showing upward mobility. For example, the tribal shawl 'Puanlaisan' for males has given way to jackets made of the same material they have become unisex, and are sold at tourist spots with its lore and history totally ignored. No doubt change is inevitable and the weaver artisan must be cognizant of and willing to adopt to modern technology to cater to market demands, but in the process, some priceless handlooms have become extinct, Other handicrafts, dance forms, musical instruments too, have been replaced by western artifacts, modern musical instruments like the guitar, pianos, violin etc. The silver gongs an important and necessary musical instrument in all celebrations has lost its importance.

Young people more attuned to a fast pace of life and competition in every sphere are easily attracted, to what is new and attractive, and inevitably they abandon many traditional forms and products. They desire to embrace the global culture without preserving what is important in their own.

Similarly traditional marriage ceremonies which once used to be simple, joyous occasions where the entire village community joined in the celebration has been replaced by the western system of wedding ceremonies. This is partly because marriages take place in Churches, as the majority of tribals are Christian. But the expenditure entailed on externals like the wedding gown, cake, etc. serve to detract from the importance of the vows exchanged at the ceremony. Moreover, as a result of exposure to the outside world the simple tribal parent is now competing with his peers to provide a marriageable daughter. With a sizeable dowry, in the form of elaborate expensive wardrobe, furniture, electronics, consumables like a car etc. This contrasts with the simple loom and agricultural implements traditionally provided to the bride by her parents on the wedding day. The expenditure involved in the entire passage of rite has increased more than tenfold in the present day and rendered many parents insolvent for the rest of their lives.

The socio-cultural changes are so rapid that the family, which is closely knit, and the practice of monogamy seem to be changing and eroding. The family economy which is shared by all the family members especially in the agricultural work is no longer so, due to modern education. The children are not taught manual labour, folktales, folksongs, the myths and customs. The whole society is becoming individualistic and the concern for the community is on the decline.[10]

Materialistic Consumerism

One impact of globalization has been the ushering in of a culture of consumerism, which tends to make people live beyond their means. The appetite for novelties continues to grow. Even in poor villages, which earlier subsisted on meals cooked from staple grains grown, is replaced by fast foods like Maggie noodles, aerated drinks like coca-cola etc, which have taken the place of traditional rice beer. These not only have harmful effects on the general health of the consumers but entail unnecessary expenses. Modern amenities and electronic goods like television, fridge, washing machine, computer and modern gadgets etc. is a must for the tribals today.

Globalisation and Cultural Change

The educated and urbanized have a tendency towards modernization and neglect their cultural ethos by the choices they make.[11] While cultural pluralism is radical, in that it rejects long established cultural traditions that the dominant as well as minority elites wish to conserve, yet cultural pluralism maybe a force for modernity because it accords a place to ethnic minority culture, that may be in certain instances be more advanced than the culture of the majority, whereas multicultarism is anti modern to the extent it stresses affirmative action.[12] Improved communications gradually weakened the microcosmic boundaries and the people were exposed to the life outside the limited local microcosmic boundaries.[13]

In almost every sphere of activity, there is a growing number of transnational organizations, linking people in transnational relations. The widespread network of international governmental organizations, combined with international non-governmental organizations (NGOs), provides the conditions for global governance. As an immediate result, people across the world have become global citizens who co-operate in different spheres to create a more just or balanced world order. They learn to think out of the box and become more open-minded. This in turn would, in course of time in relation to the tribals of Manipur, lessen ethnic tensions and usher in peace and development. The tribals are complaining about an erosion of culture under the impact of globalisation. Emergence of caste war in India in general and ethnic war particularly in Manipur is also an impact of globalisation. According to Vikeyemo Zao (filmmaker), modernity and the advent of Christianity have weakened the rich cultural ethos of the Naga tribes. Culture is a composite behavior pattern of the human being, which is given by many factors. Dynamics of cultural change is given by education, information, administration, besides the economic factors of income and social security. Culture undergoes change overtime when these perspectives change.

For a variety of historical reasons (the emergence of machines, cities, anonymity, money mass media, standardization, atomization), we have lost awareness of story-telling as a way to dramatize and order human existence. Myths and stories live in our imagination. It adds perspective and excitement to our life. Within each of us is a tribe with a complete cycle of legends and dances, songs to be sung. We are born into rich mythical lives; we need only claim the stories that are our birthright.[14] Every ethnic group developed a culture of its own in a historical setting that was hostile and lacked communication with another.[15] Although erosion of tribal culture has occurred, and efforts are on to stem further erosion, appreciation of other's cultures and absorbing what is good in them. For example Akbar's Din-i-Ilahi is equally important. Networking of cultures is a must for open societies. When one cultural entity dialogues with another cultural entity, it promotes understanding, mutual appreciation and trust.[16]

A pertinent point of debate and analysis is whether globalization is good or bad? This cannot be answered in black or white. There are several grays in between. Its positive or negative fallout depends on each country and government who draws up policies to protect their citizens from the adverse consequences by imposing sanction tariffs, etc especially in the context of the economy, Globalization is here to stay, not to simply go away. Therefore, the government needs to formulate strategies that will benefit the tribals in Manipur, breaking their isolation and affording them an equal share of the benefits.

Globalisation, which entails dissolution of the old structures and boundaries of national states and communities, and which also involves the transnationalisation of economic and cultural life has been an ongoing process in Manipur. The never-ending supply of goods from China, Thailand, Indonesia, and mainly Myanmar through Moreh, a border town situated between Manipur and Myanmar, nearly 150 Kilometres from Imphal, has made the people of Manipur come closer to the people of Myanmar, than to the rest of India.

If globalisation is conceived in terms of the creation of a global space and community, in this all will be global citizens and neighbours. Then the design is far from tailor made for the diverse ethnic groups, of more than 33 tribes, of Manipur, who are constantly engaged in a struggle for identity and land, overlapping each other, more than often than not and creating deep fissures in society and state.

The reason why globalisation is so internalised and localised in Manipur, may be because of its ability to bring the new (read international) cultural elements together with old (national, but 'local' may be the more appropriate word here) elements, without allowing the new 'synthesis' to have an overtone of either one of the two component culture. As Lal Dena comments, 'Ironically, the people also saw Christian ideas of Supreme God as referring to the Supreme Being of their animistic religion. In fact, the Christian God and the Supreme Being of their traditional religion were addressed by the same name 'Pathien'. Thus, there was the indigenous concept of the Supreme Being which was continuous in its essentials with the Christian concept.[1]

However, the effect of globalisation on market economy of the tribals favours certain communities by virtue of their strategic location and direct access to Myanmar through which most imported goods make their way to Manipur. The goods are found in greater abundance in Imphal, Chandel (Moreh comes under this district) and in Churachandpur (the largest district of Manipur), while in other areas, the impact is minimal. This does not mean that goods from countries other than S. E. Asia do not come to Manipur especially in the food section, but S. E. Asian goods predominate because of the porous border and the Government's 'Look East Policy'.

These goods include mostly everything, from rice to instant noodles, cosmetics to shampoos, T-shirts to blankets, music instruments to electronic items, toys to bicycles, and even at some stage petrol – when the price in Manipur was beyond the reach of the commoner, due to economic blockade affected by the Nagas and Kukis on the National highways. Manipur is not connected by rail to any other state in India, and all these came at a much lower price than products of MNC's located in other parts of India's. The flow of goods to and fro from Manipur via the International border while being influenced by forces of globalization, is also dependent on other factors like the degree of security on the land route, endemic bandhs, extortion on the highway, etc Particular goods are in demand in different seasons. The urge to accumulate especially the attractive plastic containers, furniture etc. often has a detrimental effect on the family purse. The gap between the 'haves' and have-nots' is widening. The city culture especially with government servants with 'westernized colouring' creates tremendous economic pressure. Monetary economy is manifestly transformed by fast money or easy money, love of material comforts, corruption and unfair means etc. Now there is a emerging a competitive, monetized new class stratified by wealth among the tribals.[17]

An MNC like 'Amways' whose products enjoy an enviable reputation worldwide came to Manipur at a time when customers who had no money for luxuries, were duped by the Amway agents into buying expensive cosmetics, medicines, nutrition supplements etc, while others were brainwashed into becoming distributors without being trained in how to sell the products. As a result many such persons were left with unsold products, their money was locked up, and the products enjoy a certain shelf like – thereafter they cannot be sold. Many young entrepreneur agents fell into debt, with no assets to invest in an alternate line of work or business.

The destruction of forms of social solidarity among the tribals of Manipur leaves a gaping hole in the social order. It then becomes peculiarly difficult to control the resultant anti-social behaviours such as criminality, pornography, or the virtual enslavement of others. The reduction of 'freedom' to 'freedom of enterprise' unleashes all those 'negative freedoms' that Polanyi saw as inextricably tied in with the positive freedoms.[18] There is a social division that is 'the have' and 'the have nots' 'educated' and 'illiterates'. In the past the wealth of a richman was counted by the number of paddy fields, cattle, lands, etc. Today the wealth of a person is seen in the building, money, vehicle, educated children etc.[19]

Through unlicensed market freedom, a rise in opium trade occurred on the borders of Manipur. This economic exchange caused a drug abuse epidemic in Manpur, which grew to such proportions that it became inextricably linked with the twin epidemic of HIV/AIDS. Despite the plethora of drug rehabilitation and drop in centres, and AIDS hospics, the incidence of drug abuse and HIV infection is escalating because of the thriving trade in narcotics, the Indo-Myanmar border is extremely porous and because of free passage across the border on the land route because of ethnic contiguity of tribes living on both sides, many individuals make their living from drug peddling and trafficking. The price of narcotics in the global market naturally influences the price at which drugs are sold in Manipur. The age of initiation into drugs use has decreased from the twenties to the teens.

Another example is the growing of poppy for economic benefit; not considering the adverse consequences that occur when poppy is refined into heroin (in refineries along the porous Indo-Myanmar border) and sold in the market. Even though the level of drug use has increased steadily in Manipur, with middle school children even succumbing to drug abuse, and despite awareness about the consequences of HIV and AIDS, heroin is a choice of drugs for many young educated tribals in Manipur. This is not to say that other communities abstain from illegal drugs.

A negative consequence of globalization on the tribals of Manipur is growing unemployment due to inability of smaller industries (basically cottage/miniscule as Manipur is a non-industrialised State) to compete with the international industrial firms, loss of livelihood for traditional artisans and craftsmen, and migration of people from their original environment to towns where prospects of livelihood are daunting. In their original habitat they enjoyed the produce of the fields, possessed their own homes where they reared livestock essential to tribal living.

Globalisation cannot be stopped but the tribals have to practice discernment in adoption of global practices/culture. They cannot blindly ape or embrace globalization, but should judiciously choose that which will enhance their lifestyle, while simultaneously permitting them to retain their own culture and practices.

Until the year 2000, AD most of the tribals who migrated to cities like Delhi, Mumbai, Bangalore etc were those working in central government jobs or those pursuing higher studies. The momentum of migration grew exponentially after 2000 AD because of disturbed conditions of law and order, which adversely impacted both education and employment and large number of tribals travelled to urban metros for schools, college, higher education and sustainable livelihood. Duration of stay in mega cities differs from community to community. Most of the student communities remain for four to five years and return home after completion of studies while those who manage to get jobs continue or migrate to other cities. Those who work in Government jobs and private sectors continue to remain until they retire and return back to their native states but this phenomenon is already changing because of violence and insecurity in the socio-political set up of Manipur.

In fact, these tribals migrants tend to form a kind of Diaspora, and it is by no means certain whether they remit even a part of their earnings to their families in Manipur. There is a simultaneous brain cum financial drain, as the diaspora having no prospects of advancement at home continue to remain in metros outside. Vast sums of money go from Manipur to finance education of its girls and boys outside, but very few returns to contribute to development in society and state in their home. Moreover, tribals having been educated in missionary schools in Manipur are usually fluent in English and are well positioned to find jobs outside.

Social-political unrest in the region includes mushrooming of groups of non-state actors, bloodshed, endemic strikes which disrupt normal life, imposition of Armed Forces Special Powers Act and the corrupt nature of government machineries, etc. These unrests have been increasing in magnitude for the last 30 years especially. There being nothing as simple as security of life, development takes a backseat in the absence of peace evident from the total absence of essential amenities like portable water, regular power supply, proper drainage, sanitation and standard metalled roads. Globalisation has channeled money into hands of non-state actors, and being armed they are at liberty to abduct, hold for ransom, kill or gift a bomb.

Until the advent of colonial rule in Manipur (1891) the tribes lived in isolation. But after Manipur's merger with revolutionary developments in transport and communication (especially regular air services), with introduction of computer technology, the tribals were catapulted into a new globalised world whose outward trappings literally mesmerised them. For instance, many young girls and boys sought employment in BPO's outside because of the higher salaries paid, as also in the aviation, hospitality and allied fields. But once settled in the metros, they are unwilling to return home. So in a few decades there will be only a very young and very old population in the state which raises the question of how these two categories of people will support themselves. The remittances home from the Manipuri diaspora would appear to be minimal although no statistical analysis is available.

Lack of employment opportunities in the state is a major push factor of migration to other mega cities. Government employment is open to not people of merit but to those who wield the power of money, exert muscle power and access to the power that be. The educated poor, who lack such advantages, have no hope for government employment. It is not that corruption and nepotism is a new phenomena in Manipur, but its pace has accelerated with globalization.

Private sectors enterprise and non-governmental business establishments are few operating on miniscule capital and unable to provide employment, even to those eminently qualified for the task. Because of constant threats and intimidations, they often fold up. An offshoot of globalization is an entrenched culture of violence. The high level of military presence, terrorism, seditious literature, spread of disaffection, illegal immigration, trafficking in narcotics, explosive manufacturing, smuggling contraband goods, counterfeiting currency, money laundering, corruption, fraudulent withdrawals of money that is meant for infrastructure developments, high handedness of politicians- all these are responsible for nurturing the culture of violence. All these forces have made the North-East, a theatre for entertainment, which impedes growth. There is hardly any rule of law.[20]

Another causative factor for migration is the educational system, which is riddled with problems. Almost all government-run schools are non-functional as illustrated by poor results at the time of examination. Other evils also pervade the system: in the year 2010 for 100 days no classes were held following an incident of merciless killing of two civilians by the police. Inevitably, Parents, who are in any position to afford to, send their children for better education outside. But in the guise of providing a good education, many individuals, agents and institutions are targeting innocent children and indulging in human trafficking where focus is on money gained through the enterprise. Despite enaction of strict laws, the trade in flesh trade continues, as poor families are easily called into giving up their children to people who promise them a better life. Moreover, in the echelons of higher education, Manipur lags behind, despite having 2 universities, 2 Institutes of Medical science, technical institutions etc. The best (brilliant) students tend to migrate to other cities to pursue higher studies and gain meaningful employment.

Every individual would like to own and use if not an automobile, at least a two-wheeler, and since the roads have not been expanded to meet the needs of more drivers on the road, the pollution and noise decibels caused by fumes emitted and constant pressing of the horn has gone beyond bearable limits. The acceleration of the consumerist tendency has resulted in the desire of individuals to own some form of transport, whether it be a car, SUV, motorcycle etc. Moreover, with the liberation of the economy, banks are giving loans on an easy basis for purchase of the same. This has resulted in congestion on all major as well as minor roads, traffic snarls, bickering, accidents, and pollution as a result of fumes emitted by vehicles. Constant horn blowing also adversely impacts hearing, whereas the automobile pollution has resulted in a high increase in respiratory diseases, specially asthma in children.

People as a whole seem to show a marked preference for an affluent lifestyle, and in the process, have developed some non-traditional, unsavory characteristics and behavior as for example trafficking young children, both boys and girls to unlicensed children's homes in South India, for supposedly a free education. The individuals involved in this trade as reported in state dailies are mainly tribal Christians who have established links with Christian pastors in the South. Most of the children aged between 7-13 years are abused, mentally and physically, and are often made to do jobs like carpentry, cooking and laundry.

There have been cases of children dying under suspicious circumstances, even though at the time of their departure from the state, the person accompanying the children collects anything between ₹ 10,000 to ₹ 15,000 from each child's family. The rescue of 76 malnourished children, from Manipur and Assam, from a home at Kuzhithurai in Kanyakumari district is only the tip of the vast network, which receives crores of rupees from Churches and agencies abroad by showing a large number of children under their care. Incidentally, a majority of homes charged with trafficking are run by missionaries or evangelical societies. "These institutions exploit religion to make money. With many of them not registered with the government, the homes escape scrutiny," says Vidya Reddy of Tulir, Centre for Prevention and Healing of Child Sexual Abuse. Before the advent of modernization such activities as trafficking of children for monetary gain would never have crossed the mind of simple tribal people.

With new definitions of ethnicity and nationalism emerging, and the struggle for sovereign or autonomous states by several ethnic minorities e.g. (Serbs, Bosnians, South Sudan etc.) Manipur too has been impacted by this offshoot of globalization. Factional feuds and insurgent activities have decimated villages, communities, and becoming a major deterrent to development. Some fortunate survivors migrate and carve out a new life for themselves in urban centres outside.

Migration is the barometer of changing socio-economic and political conditions at the National and International levels. It is also a sign of wide disparities in economic and social conditions between the origin and destination. Migration and development is a growing area of interest. There has been much debate on the negative impact of migration on development and vice versa. On the one hand, it is argued that underdevelopment is a cause of migration, and on the other hand, globalization also leads to migration.

CONCLUSION

Globalisation makes people global citizens, multi-cultural persons who are at ease in any situation/place and who being able to think out of the box have established contacts across the globe not only in personal but inter-personal relationships. Globalisation's impact has raised the confidence levels especially of youth who have greater aspirations from the future armed as they are with new knowledge and skills. Simultaneously it creates disenchantment with village life- the old way of living, celebrating etc becomes passé and induces migration to urban centres even outside of Manipur. And once settled outside, they are reluctant to return. They also do not remit money back home, as cost of living is higher in urban metros.

REFERENCES

1. Sacks, L.Howard, *The Dignity of Difference*, Urbana University of Illinois Press, 2003. p. 26.
2. Rangarajan, in *Outlook* on Globalisation, 15 January 2007.
3. *Newsweek*, 6 June 2011.
4. Friedman, Thomas L., *The World is Flat: The Globalised World in the 21st Century*, Farrer, Straus & Giroux, 2005. p. 237.
5. Dissanayake, Wimal and K. Moti Gokulsing, *Popular Culture in a Globalised India*, Routledge, Ahingdom Oxon, 1988. p. 45.
6. Hudson, T. C., *The Meitheis*. Low Price Publications, Delhi. Reprinted 2007. p. 40.
7. Jeyaseelan, L., Relevance of the Print Media in the Cultural Context of Northeast India, in L. Jayaseelan (Ed.), *Culture, Mission and Contetualisation*. p. 117.
8. Friedman, A. Thomas, *The World is Flat, op. cit.* p. 87.
9. Jeyaseelan, Quoting Jacob Srampicral a Leena Joseph (Eds.), Priorities and Strategies. A report of the Mussoorie Consultation, 1995. p. 5.
10. Nepuni, William, *Socio-Cultural History of Shupfomei Naga Tribe*, Mittal Publications, New Delhi, 2010. p. 181.
11. Jeyaselan, *Ibid.* p. 183.

12. Safran, William, "Non-Separatist Politics Regarding Ethnic minority; Positive Approaches and Ambiguous Consequences," *International Political Science Review*, 15:1 (1994). pp. 61-80.
13. *Journal of the International African Institute*, Vol. 45 no. 31975, p. 220.
14. Noll, Ray and Noll, Jean, *The Family Book of People*, Indiana – Our Sunday Visitor Inc. 1981. p. 77.
15. Jeyaselan, *Ibid.* p. 188.
16. Jeyaselan, *op. cit.* p. 189.
17. Nepuni, William, *Socio-Cultural History of Shupfomei Naga Tribe*, p. 187.
18. *Op. cit.* p. 185.
19. William Nepuni, p. 186.
20. Jeyasaleen, *op. cit.* p. 190.

Conclusion

Modernisation of the tribals community was basically initiated by the Christian missionaries who were supported by the British colonialists. However some attempts to introduce western education had been made prior to the establishment of colonial rule in 1891, but they were not successful. The process of momentum was accelerated in the twentieth century when Manipur joined the Indian Union, which entailed introducing the Indian Government system of formal education, as also a result of the rise of an educated elite middle class, because of inculturation and a sense of mission, as also the impact of a global culture.

There are 33 recognised tribes in Manipur who can be broadly classified into 2 groups- Naga and Kuki-Chin. Although initially the tribals resisted conversion to Christianity, the concept of eternal life, as also the changes ushered in every sphere won over the tribals who converted en masse to Christianity. Christianity besides offering spiritual succor lifted the tribals from the old world to the new and set them on the path of development and progress, by arousing them from their isolation and providing a more holistic world view. Besides the tribals fluency in English language as a result of gospel teaching as also their formal education gave them a distinct advantage which leads to the growth of middle class elite which dominated the fields of politics, culture, religion and economy. But Christianity and western education initially adversely affected tribal culture in that it condemned and destroyed much of the rich cultural heritage. But by the later part of the 20th century, a new realization of adopting Christianity to its tribal milieu dawned and a process of inculturation and adjustment followed. This was facilitated by the local missionaries who made an all out attempt to root Christianity in its tribal milieu.

In the initial phase of evangelization the Christian missionaries had ridden rough-shot on the sentiments and culture of the tribals. But to make Christianity deep rooted, they changed their perspective, gradually, they engaged in an encounter and engagement with cultures, and so became a more effective instrument of Mission. The process of inculturation was facilitated by indigenous Christian tribals especially, priests, pastors, nuns, catechists. The church promotes both pluralities as also harmonious co-operation among tribes, ushering in an atmosphere of peace. Tradition has combined with modernity in the integration of the social perspective of the tribals with the Gospel perspective. Contextualisation ensures that the ways people communicate with one another are used in communication of the Gospel and in the new church structures, customs and rituals.

Another important reason for modernization was education-it moulded the society anew. Initially there was hostility towards the educators because of mistaken perception on the impact of education. Very soon this perception changed especially because of the attitude of the missionaries to the tribals, their conversion to Christianity and the opportunities especially for livelihood that were made available, and the indifferent attitude of the

Manipur Government towards the tribals. The missionaries' mission was that in order to understand the Gospel an individual must know how to read. It also resulted in the growth of women's education and establishment of women's societies.

As a result of education, the tribals moved forth quickly in the path of modernization. Not only literacy marked a quick growth- the trajectory of development impact on material conditions and way of life, leading to transformation in the sphere of politics, governance, festivals, feasts, song, dance, social structure and economy. It facilitated their entry into central and state governance services and many of the leading IAS, IPS, officers in Manipur owe their success to missionary education. Education also rid them of many superstitious beliefs and practices, and they adopted a new value system, and world view as a result of emerging from the isolation of their mountain fastness.

One inadvertent result of the advent of Christianity and the impact of colonial rule coupled with modern education was the emergence of a middle class in the formerly egalitarian social set-up of the tribals. This middle class emerged from the lower rungs of the social order but quickly rose to a position of predominance, cornering positions and posts in governance, politics, religion, economy, society. They also tore asunder the bars of isolation and allowed the tribals to imbibe new values and perspectives, without however denigrating their own culture. The new middle class rallied around the missionaries not their traditional chiefs, and the British administrators utilized the services of Christian tribals, undermining the prerogatives of the Chiefs. Urbanisation also facilitated the rise of the middle class, which in course of time became stratified. The middle class also began to lead the ethnic movements aimed at achieving a homeland, and asserted a distinct sense of militant nationalism. A plethora of militant organizations came into being.

Globalisation impacted the tribals in many ways on their quest for modernization. It led to large scale migration of the tribals from the hill areas to the plains, establishment of colonies in urban areas christened after them, increased urbanization, greater job opportunities and accelerated connectivity. They became a part of the global culture. It also led to monetization of the economy, shift to cash crop cultivation and quality control in the manufacture of consumer goods, where traditional goods were integrated with modern concepts of design and production. It has also inculcated a scientific temperament and a liberal attitude to developments in the field of science and technology and inculcated a consciousness of human rights.

But globalization has eroded the community-based economy of the tribals, and created stratification in the formerly egalitarian tribal society which led to an increase of individualism and a glaring consumerism, as also erosion of tribal culture; increase in the cost of living, divisions in society leading to ethnic consciousness and strife. Globalisation has also been facilitated by the porous Indo-Myanmar border in Manipur, which is a conduit for goods coming from all over South East Asia. It has also facilitated a flourishing trade in illicit drugs accompanied by the twin epidemics of drug abuse and HIV/AIDS and enlarged poppy cultivation. Loss of livelihoods has resulted from displacement of indigenous products by those produced by MNC's. There is also a constant migration to other cities, states, countries and the tribal diaspora means an intellectual cum monetary drain for Manipur, as the best and brightest seek employment outside. Also remittances from them to the state are scanty.

An adverse consequences of globalization are an escalation of violence, trafficking in human beings, especially children and women hailing from tribal communities, road and traffic congestion, rise in pollution, rise in disease (e.g. Asthma) rise in factional feuds coupled with insurgency.

Of all the factors that modernised the tribals, Christianity and western education had the greatest impact, but the rise of the middle class, led to tribal movements aimed at creation of independent homelands.

Bibliography

Aloysius, Nehkhojang T., The Socio-Cultural life of the Zomis of Manipur. In L. Jayaseelan (Ed.), *Culture, Mission and Contextualization*. Catholic Manipur Publications, 2000.

Anikuzhikattil, J. G. Palackapapillel, J. Puthenpurakal – *Understanding Tribal Cultures for effective education*, Shillong, 2003.

Archbishop Joseph Mittathany DD, *Churches Pastoral Approach to Culture, Mission and Contextualization*. Catholic Manipur Publications, 2000.

Allen, B. C., *Gazetteer of Naga Hills and Manipur*, Mittal Publication, 1905.

Basanta, N., *Socio-Economic Change in Manipur 1891-1947*, Imphal, 1998.

Brown. R., *Statistical Account of Manipur*, Mittal Publication, New Delhi, 2001.

Bromley, David B., & Dennis Basil Bromley, *The Psychology of Human Aging*, Penguin Group, New Zealand, Revised, 1974.

Carey, S. Bertram and Tuck H. N., *The Chin Hills Vol. I & II*, Firma KLM Calcutta, 1976 reprinted.

Chaube, Shibani Kinkar, *Hill Politics in Northeast India*, Orient Longman, Calcutta, 1973.

Champang, J., *Christian Life in a Tribal Context in Manipur*, Ukhrul, 1990.

Dissanayake, Wimal & K. Moti Gokulsing, *Popular Culture in a Globalised India*. Routledge, Ahingdom Oxon. 1988.

Dun, E. W., *Gazetteer of Manipur*, Mittal Publication, New Delhi, 1981. Reproduced.

Downs, Frederick, *Social Movements Among Tribes of India – Essays on Christianity in North East India*, Delhi, 1983.

Downs, F. S., *The Mighty Works of God*, Christian Literature Centre, Pan Bazaar, Gauhati, 1971.

Das, S. T., *Tribal Life of North-East India*, Delhi, 1986.

Devi, Jamini, *Education in Manipur*, Imphal, 1989.

Friedman, Thomas A. L., *The World is Flat: The Globalised World in the 21st Century*, Farrer, Straus & Giroux 2005, First Edition.

Fernandes, Leela, *India's New Middle Class: Democratic Politics in an Era of Economic Reform*. University of Minnesota Press, 2006.

Foreword Report of Most Rev. Joseph Mittathany D. D., Archbishop of Imphal, in L. Jayaseelan (Ed.), *Culture, Mission and Contextualization*, 2000.

Gellner Ernest Andre, *Nations and Nationalism: New Perspectives on the Past Series*, Publisher Ithaca, NY Cornell University Press, 1988.

Gori, Gulab Khan, *Changing Phase of Tribal Area of Manipur*, Delhi, 1984.

Gangte, T. S., *The Kukis of Manipur*, Gyan Publishing House, New Delhi, 2nd Edition, 2003.

Guite, K. P., 'Development of Education in the Hill Areas of Manipur'. Unpublished thesis submitted to Manipur University, 1991.

Gollius, A. A. (Ed.), *Rome*, Pontifical Gregorian University, 1983.

Goswami, Tarun, *Kuki Life and Lore*, Haflong, 1985.

Horam, M., *Naga Polity*, Delhi, 1975.

Horam, M., *The Rising Nagas*. Vivek Publishing House, Delhi, 1974.

Haokip, Peter, Folk Culture: A Medium for the Spread of the Gospel in *Culture, Mission and Contextualization*, Catholic Manipur Publications, 2000.

Haokip, Holkhongam, 'Christian Missionaries Among the Kukis: A Historical Study'. Unpublished Ph.D thesis submitted to Manipur University, 2009.

Herskovits, Melville J., *Cultural Anthropology*, Oxford and IBH Publication, New Delhi, 1954.

Haokip, Seilen Dr., *Rhetorics of Kuki Nationalism, A Treatise*, Lustra Print, New Delhi, 2010.

Hudson, T. C., *The Meitheis*, Low Price Publications, Delhi. Reprinted, 2007.

Haokip, P. S., *Zale'n-gam: The Kuki Nation*, Kuki National Organisation, Zale'n-gam, 2008, (Rev. ed.).

Irene Salam, "Socio and Cultural Life of the Tribals before the Advent of Christianity," cit S. Karotemprel, *The Impact of Christianity on the Tribals of North East India*, Manipur University, 2000.

Irene, Salam, "The Attitude of the Catholic Church towards Society and State in Manipur," cit. Fr. M. C. George, Rector Don Bosco, Imphal. Manipur University, 2000.

Irene, Salam, *Catholic Education in Manipur*, Scholars Publishing House, New Delhi, 2006.

Imotemjen, Aier K., *A Chance for the Church*, Guwahati, 1982.

Imchen, C. L., *The Nagas and the Legacy of Civilizing Mission of the Western World*, 1995.

Jayaseelan, L., *Impact of the Missionary Movement in Manipur*, Scholar Publishing House, Delhi, 1996.

Jayaseelan, L. (Ed.), Dr. Kamei Gailangam and Dr. Gina Shangkham, *Change and Continuity in the Tribal Society of Manipur*.

Jamkhothang, Rev. T., *"A proposed Guidance of the North East India General Mission on Schools."* An unpublished Bachelor of *Divinity* thesis Serampore Theological College, 1963.

Johnstone, James Sir, *Manipur and Nagas*, Gyan Publishing House, 2002.

Jonah, M. S. and Mahangthei, K. (ed.), *Forty Years in Manipur*, Assam (An Account of the work of W. Pettigrew, the first foreign Missionary in Manipur landed in 1894, Imphal), 1986.

Kabui, Gangmumei, *The History of Zeliangrong Nagas from Makhel to Rani Gaidinliu*, Spectrum Publications, Guwahati, 2000.

Kabui, Gangmumei, *Philosophy of History and Historiography of Manipur*, Akansha Publishing House, 2006.

Kipgen, Mangkhosat, *Christianity and Mizo Culture*, Published by the Author at Assam Printing Works (P) Jorhat, Assam, 1997.

Kedourie, Elie, *Nationalism*, Wiley-Blackwell, Fourth Expanded Edition, 1993.

Kipgen, Donn Morgan, 2006, *The Great Betrayal: Brief Notes on Kuki Insurgency Movement*. http://manipuronline.com

Khaizalian, D., *Taangthupha Tunma leh Tunung*, Published at Lamka, 1986.

Karotemprel, Sebastian, 'The Impact of Christianity on the Tribes of North East India' in Sarthak Sengupta (Ed.), *the Tribal Situation in North East India*, Inter India Publication, New Delhi, 1994.

Lyngdoh Sylvanus Sngi, 'The Tribal Value System and the Impact of Christianity on it'. In J. Puthenpurakal (Ed.) *Impact of Christianity on North East India*, Vendrame Institute Publications, Shillong, 1996.

Lolly, R. R., *The Baptist Church in Manipur*, Imphal, 1985.

Dena, Lal, *Christian Missions and Colonialism*, Published by Vendrame Institute, Shillong, 1988.

Dena, Lal, *History of Modern Manipur:1826-1946*, Orbit Publishers, New Delhi, 1991.

Lewis, C. S. cit. in R. Vashum, *Nagas Right for Self Determination*, Mittal Publications, New Delhi, 2000.

Luikham, T., *A Short History of the Manipur Baptist Christian Golden Jubilee*, Imphal, 1984.

Lalhmuoklien, Rev. (Dr.), *Gospel Through Darkness: History and Missionary Work of the North East India General Mission (ECCI) 1910-2004.*

Neli, Linus, 'In Search of Christ Experience through Culture', Jayaseelan, L. (Ed.), *Culture, Mission and Contextualization*, 2000.

Melville J. Herskarts, *Cultural Anthropology*, (New Delhi, Oxford 1947). Mackenzie, A., *The North East Frontier of Bengal*, Mittal Publication, New Delhi. Reproduced, 2005.

Manjaly, Thomas Dr., 'Inculturating the Gospel: Some Biblical Models' in Jayaseelan, L., *Culture, Mission and Contextualization*, Catholic Manipur Publications, 2000.

Mukhim, Patricia, 'Christian Impact on North East India and National Integration' in Puthenpurakal, J. (Ed.), *Impact of Christianity on North East India*, Vendrame Institute Publications, Shillong, 1996.

Nag, Sajal, 'Naga Identity: Formation, Construction and Expansion' in C. J. Thomas and Gurudas Das (Ed.), *Dimensions of Development in Nagaland*, Regency Publications, New Delhi, 2002.

Nunthara, C., *Understanding Tribal Culture*, Mizoram, 1999.

Noll, Ray and Noll, Jean, *The Family Book of People Indiana*, Our Sunday Visitor Inc., 1981.

Nepuni, William, *Socio-Cultural History of Shupfomei Naga Tribe*, Mittal Publications, New Delhi, 2010.

Pudaite, Jonathan, *The Legacy of Watkin R. Roberts: The Pioneer Missionary who advocated and Empowered Indigenous Christian Leader*, Partnership Publication, Shillong, 2009.

Ray, B. Datta, *Tribal Identity and Tension in North East India*, Omsons Publications, 1989.

Pulamte, John H., 'Development of Education in Churachandpu District.' (with Special reference to the Hmars). Unpublished Ph.D thesis submitted to Manipur University, 2002.

Report of Rev. Basil E. Jones submitted to the Mission Committee at Liverpool as a basis for discussion on the future educational policy to be pursued in Lushai hills (1924-1947) in Lal Dena Christian Missions and Colonialism, 1988.

Ruivah, Khashim, *Social Change among the Nagas (Tangkhuls)*, Cosmo Publication, Delhi, 1993.

Ray, Asok Kumar, *Authority and Legitimacy: A Study of the Thadou-Kukis in Manipur*, Renaissance Publishing House, Delhi, 1990.

Shishak, Reverend (Dr.) Tuisem A., "Nagas and Education" in *Nagas at Work*, NSUD Publication, New Delhi, 1996.

Singh, L. Leiren,'Reverend William Pettigrew and Modern Education in Manipur, in *Pettigrew Centenary Celebrations Committee Manipur*, 1996.

Singh, N. Joykumar, *Social Movements in Manipur*, Mittal Publication, New Delhi, 2005.

Sacks, L. Howard, *The Dignity of Difference*. Urbana University of Illinois Press, 2003.

Sena, Lalremchuani, *The Mizo Independence Movement*, unpublished M.A. Dissertation submitted to the Californian State University, 1974.

Smith, A., Anthony, *National Identity*, Penguin, London, 1991.

Singh, A. Koireng, *Ethnicity and Inter-Community Conflicts: A Case of Kuki-Naga in Manipur*, Akansha Publishing House, New Delhi, 2008.

Singh, S. Mangi, The Kuki-Paite Clash (1997-98) in Manipur, in N. Joykumar Singh (Ed.), *Ethnic Relations among the People of North-East India*, Centre for Manipur Studies, Manipur University and Akansha Publishing House, New Delhi, 2006.

Sachidanand, *Cultural Changes in Tribal Bihar*, Calcutta, 1964.

Stracey, P. D., *Nagaland Nightmare*, Allied Publishers, New Delhi, 1968,

Soaras, G. M., – *Prabhu, Tribal Values in India*, Jeevadhaea, 1994.

Shakespeare, Major J., *History of Assam Rifles*, Cultural Publishing House, 1922.

Singh, Prakash, *Nagaland*, National Book Trust, New Delhi. 1995. (4th ed.)

Shimray, R. R., *Origin and Culture of Nagas*, Delhi, 1985.

Shimray, Ayai, 'Revd. William Pettigrew and his times 1869-1943' unpublished Ph.D. thesis submitted to Manipur University, 2006.

Thanzaua, C.F. & R. L. Hnuni, 'Ethnicity, Identity and Humanities: On India tribal perspective', in M. G. Brett (Ed.) *Ethnicity and the Bible*, New York. 1996.

The Epistle to Diognets quoted in G. M. Soares, *Prabhu*, 1976.

Vashum, R., *Nagas: Right to Self Determination*, Mittal Publication, New Delhi, 2000.

Vaiphei, Rev. S. Prim, 'The Kukis' in Sanajaoba (Ed), *Manipur Past and Present*, Vol. 3, Mittal Publication, New Delhi, 1995.

Vaiphei, Rev. S. Prim, *Different Cultural Practices among the Christians in Manipur*, Imphal, 1980.

Wallerstein, Immanuel, *Social Change, The colonial Situation*, John Wiley and Sons, INC, New York, 1966.

Zarzolien, 'Religious Beliefs and Practices Among the Hmars through the Ages'. Unpublished thesis submitted to Manipur University, 1987.

Zarzolien, *The U-Now People*, Churachandpur, 1981.

JOURNALS/ MAGAZINE/SOUVENIR

Administrative Report of the Manipur Political Agency 1897-98.

Administrative Report of the Manipur Political Agency. 1937-38.

Bradshaw, Bruce, "Integrity and Respect Are Keys to Muslim Witness", *EMQ*, October 1988.

Chinzakham L. Ngaihte, "Is Our Future Hopeful?" *In the Young Paite Association Annual Magazine*. 1982, Vol. II.

Gospel Centenary Souvenir 1910-2010: Published by Celebration Committee, Churachandpur.

Journal of the International African Institute, Vol. 45 No. 3, 1975.

Kozlov, M. A. Paleobiology Database. *Paleontological Journal* 7, 1974.

Kristien, Vol. III, No. 1 February 1960. p. 1. (A Monthly Magazine Published by Independent Church of India, Churachandpur).

Newsweek, 6 June 2011.

Rangarajan, in *The Economic Times*: "Good governance key to Growth," 15th January 2009.

Safran, William, "Non-Separatist Politics regarding Ethnic-Minority; Positive Approaches and Ambiguous Consequences," *International Political Science Review*, 1994.

Songtal Village Souvenir, Churachandpur (1902-88),

Teeter, David, "Dynamic Equivalence Conversion for Tentative Muslim Believers", *Missiology*, Vol. XVIII, No. 3 July, 1990.

Index